Kaplan Publishing are constantly finding nev
looking for exam success and our online res
extra dimension to your studies.

This book comes with free MyKaplan online
study anytime, anywhere. **This free online**
separately and is included in the price of the book.

Having purchased this book, you have access to the following online study materials:

CONTENT	AAT	
	Text	Kit
Electronic version of the book	✓	✓
Knowledge Check tests with instant answers	✓	
Mock assessments online	✓	✓
Material updates	✓	✓

How to access your online resources

Received this book as part of your Kaplan course?
If you have a MyKaplan account, your full online resources will be added automatically, in line with the
information in your course confirmation email. If you've not used MyKaplan before, you'll be sent an activation
email once your resources are ready.

Bought your book from Kaplan?
We'll automatically add your online resources to your MyKaplan account. If you've not used MyKaplan before,
you'll be sent an activation email.

Bought your book from elsewhere?
Go to **www.mykaplan.co.uk/add-online-resources**
Enter the ISBN number found on the title page and back cover of this book.
Add the unique pass key number contained in the scratch panel below.
You may be required to enter additional information during this process to set up or confirm your account
details.

This code can only be used once for the registration of this book online. This registration and your online
content will expire when the examinations covered by this book have taken place. Please allow one hour from
the time you submit your book details for us to process your request.

Please scratch the film to access your unique code.

Please be aware that this code is case-sensitive and you will need
to include the dashes within the passcode, but not when entering
the ISBN.

PUBLISHING

CREDIT AND DEBT MANAGEMENT

STUDY TEXT

Qualifications and Credit Framework

Q2022

This Study Text supports study for the following AAT qualifications:

AAT Level 4 Diploma in Professional Accounting

AAT Diploma in Professional Accounting at SCQF Level 8

KAPLAN PUBLISHING'S STATEMENT OF PRINCIPLES

LINGUISTIC DIVERSITY, EQUALITY AND INCLUSION

We are committed to diversity, equality and inclusion and strive to deliver content that all users can relate to.

We are here to make a difference to the success of every learner.

Clarity, accessibility and ease of use for our learners are key to our approach.

We will use contemporary examples that are rich, engaging and representative of a diverse workplace.

We will include a representative mix of race and gender at the various levels of seniority within the businesses in our examples to support all our learners in aspiring to achieve their potential within their chosen careers.

Roles played by characters in our examples will demonstrate richness and diversity by the use of different names, backgrounds, ethnicity and gender, with a mix of sexuality, relationships and beliefs where these are relevant to the syllabus.

It must always be obvious who is being referred to in each stage of any example so that we do not detract from clarity and ease of use for each of our learners.

We will actively seek feedback from our learners on our approach and keep our policy under continuous review. If you would like to provide any feedback on our linguistic approach, please use this form (you will need to enter the link below into your browser).

https://forms.gle/U8oR3abiPpGRDY158

We will seek to devise simple measures that can be used by independent assessors to randomly check our success in the implementation of our Linguistic Equality, Diversity and Inclusion Policy.

British Library Cataloguing-in-Publication Data

A catalogue record for this book is available from the British Library.

Published by
Kaplan Publishing UK
Unit 2, The Business Centre
Molly Millars Lane
Wokingham
Berkshire
RG41 2QZ

ISBN 978-1-83996-578-4

The text in this material and any others made available by any Kaplan Group company does not amount to advice on a particular matter and should not be taken as such. No reliance should be placed on the content as the basis for any investment or other decision or in connection with any advice given to third parties. Please consult your appropriate professional adviser as necessary. Kaplan Publishing Limited and all other Kaplan group companies expressly disclaim all liability to any person in respect of any losses or other claims, whether direct, indirect, incidental, consequential or otherwise arising in relation to the use of such materials.

CONTENTS

KAPLAN PUBLISHING

INTRODUCTION

HOW TO USE THESE MATERIALS

These Kaplan Publishing learning materials have been carefully designed to make your learning experience as easy as possible and to give you the best chance of success in your AAT assessments.

They contain a number of features to help you in the study process.

The sections on the Unit Guide, the Assessment and Study Skills should be read before you commence your studies.

They are designed to familiarise you with the nature and content of the assessment and to give you tips on how best to approach your studies.

STUDY TEXT

This study text has been specially prepared for the revised AAT qualification introduced in 2022.

It is written in a practical and interactive style:

- key terms and concepts are clearly defined

- all topics are illustrated with practical examples with clearly worked solutions based on sample tasks provided by the AAT in the new examining style

- frequent activities throughout the chapters ensure that what you have learnt is regularly reinforced

- 'examination tips' help you avoid commonly made mistakes and help you focus on what is required to perform well in your examination

- 'Test your understanding' activities are included within each chapter to apply your learning and develop your understanding.

ICONS

The study chapters include the following icons throughout.

They are designed to assist you in your studies by identifying key definitions and the points at which you can test yourself on the knowledge gained.

 Definition

These sections explain important areas of Knowledge which must be understood and reproduced in an assessment.

 Example

The illustrative examples can be used to help develop an understanding of topics before attempting the activity exercises.

 Test your understanding

These are exercises which give the opportunity to assess your understanding of all the assessment areas.

 Foundation activities

These are questions to help ground your knowledge and consolidate your understanding on areas you're finding tricky.

 Extension activities

These questions are for if you're feeling confident or wish to develop your higher level skills.

Quality and accuracy are of the utmost importance to us so if you spot an error in any of our products, please send an email to mykaplanreporting@kaplan.com with full details, or follow the link to the feedback form in MyKaplan.

Our Quality Co-ordinator will work with our technical team to verify the error and take action to ensure it is corrected in future editions.

KAPLAN PUBLISHING

Progression

There are two elements of progression that we can measure: first how quickly students move through individual topics within a subject; and second how quickly they move from one course to the next. We know that there is an optimum for both, but it can vary from subject to subject and from student to student. However, using data and our experience of student performance over many years, we can make some generalisations.

A fixed period of study set out at the start of a course with key milestones is important. This can be within a subject, for example 'I will finish this topic by 30 June', or for overall achievement, such as 'I want to be qualified by the end of next year'.

Your qualification is cumulative, as earlier papers provide a foundation for your subsequent studies, so do not allow there to be too big a gap between one subject and another.

We know that exams encourage techniques that lead to some degree of short term retention, the result being that you will simply forget much of what you have already learned unless it is refreshed (look up Ebbinghaus Forgetting Curve for more details on this). This makes it more difficult as you move from one subject to another: not only will you have to learn the new subject, you will also have to relearn all the underpinning knowledge as well. This is very inefficient and slows down your overall progression which makes it more likely you may not succeed at all.

In addition, delaying your studies slows your path to qualification which can have negative impacts on your career, postponing the opportunity to apply for higher level positions and therefore higher pay.

You can use the following diagram showing the whole structure of your qualification to help you keep track of your progress.

You can use the following diagram showing the whole structure of your qualification to help you keep track of your progress.

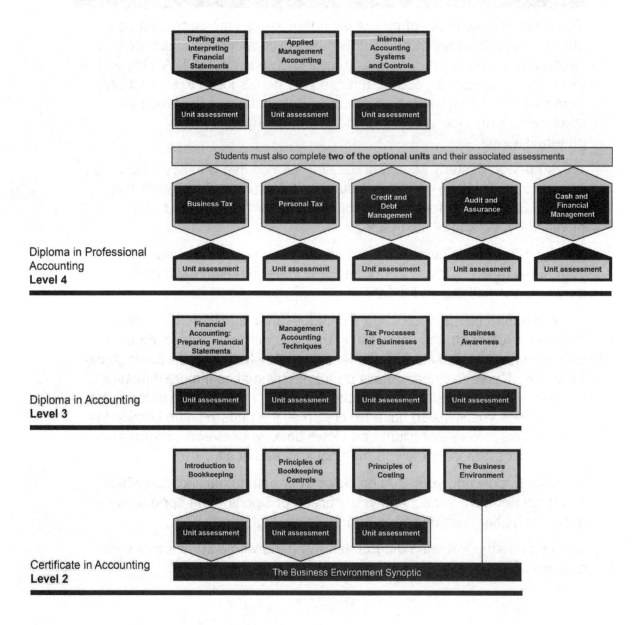

UNIT GUIDE

Introduction

This unit provides an understanding and application of the principles of effective credit control systems, including appropriate debt management systems. Organisations will usually offer credit terms to its customers, which could lead to financial difficulties if customers pay late or do not pay at all. It is therefore important to determine that potential credit customers can honour any credit terms agreed.

This unit will consider the techniques that can be used to access credit risks in line with policies, relevant legislation and ethical principles. Equally, once the credit decision has been approved, it will be important to ensure that any debts due from the customer are paid within the terms agreed. Students will also consider what techniques are used to enable the collection of any overdue debts, following organisational policies, legal procedures and methods for collecting debts.

Knowledge and use of performance measures relating to liquidity, profitability and gearing are fundamental to this unit. Students will also develop their understanding of liquidity management, bankruptcies and insolvencies, as well as the mechanisms of invoice discounting, factoring and credit insurance.

Credit and Debt Management is an **optional** unit.

Learning outcomes

- Understand relevant legislation and contract law that impacts the credit control environment.

- Understand how information is used to assess credit risk and grant credit in compliance with organisational policies and procedures.

- Understand the organisation's credit control processes for managing and collecting debts.

- Understand different techniques available to collect debts.

KAPLAN PUBLISHING

Scope of content

To perform this unit effectively you will need to know and understand the following:

Chapter

1 Understand relevant legislation and contract law that impacts the credit control environment

1.1 Statute and contract law applicable to credit control   1

Learners need to understand:

- Essential features and terminology of contract law: offer (includes invitation to treat and counter offer), acceptance, intention to create legal relations, consideration (sufficiency, adequacy and past), capacity and consent

- Legislation relating to trade descriptions, unfair contract terms, the sale and supply of goods and services and consumer credit.

1.2 Breach of contract and the circumstances in which they can be used effectively   1

Learners need to:

- Understand key considerations for breach of contract: express terms, implied terms, conditions, warranties, damages, specific performance, quantum meruit and action for price

- Understand statutory remedies for late payments of commercial debts (interest)

- Understand remedies available for collection of outstanding amounts

- Calculate interest and/or compensation due on overdue debts using statutory remedies for late payments of commercial debts.

		Chapter
1.3	**Terms and conditions associated with customer contracts**	1

Learners need to understand:

- Void, voidable and unenforceable contracts

- Retention of title clauses

1.4	**Data protection and ethical considerations associated with credit control activities**	1

Learners need to understand:

- The legislation relating to data protection

- The effect of data protection on the organisation and its customers

- Professional ethics in the context of credit control.

2 **Understand how information is used to assess credit risk and grant credit in compliance with organisational policies and procedures**

2.1	**Sources of credit status and assessment methods used in granting credit**	2

Learners need to understand:

- The range of internal and external sources of information:

    - External sources: credit agencies, trade and bank references, published financial statements, management accounts, publications and credit circles

    - Internal sources: records, conversations, emails, staff visits, calculation of performance indicators, credit scoring of performance indicators

- The useful and appropriateness of the different types of information.

2.2 Credit status of existing and potential customers using relevant ratios and performance indicators

Learners need to:

- Understand the signs of overtrading

- Understand the implications of overtrading

- Be able to analyse performance indicators of existing credit customers and/or potential credit customers

- Calculate liquidity indicators:

  - Current ratio = current assets/current liabilities = X:1

  - Quick ratio (acid test) = (current assets – inventories)/current liabilities = X:1

  - Trade receivables collection period (days) = trade receivables/revenue × 365

  - Trade payables payment period (days) = trade payables/ cost of sales × 365

  - Inventory holding period (days) = inventories/ cost of sales × 365

- Calculate profitability indicators:

  - Gross profit margin = gross profit/ revenue × 100%

  - Operating profit margin = operating profit/ revenue × 100%

  - Interest cover = operating profit/finance costs (i.e. interest) = X times

  - Return on capital employed (ROCE) = operating profit/capital employed × 100%

  - Capital employed = total equity + non-current liabilities

- Calculate debt indicators (gearing):

  - Gearing = total debt/(total debt + total equity) × 100%. Total debt is all non-current liabilities only.

Chapter

- Calculate the working capital cycle

  - Working capital cycle (days) = inventory holding period + trade receivable collection period – trade payables payment period.

2.3	**Reasons for granting, refusing, amending or extending credit**	2

Learners need to understand:

- Organisational policies and procedures specific to changes to credit terms

- How to assess and communicate changes to credit terms

- Threats to objectivity that may exist when deciding whether to grant, refuse, amend or extend credit.

3   **Understand the organisation's credit control processes for managing and collecting debts**

3.1   **Methods for the management of debts**   2, 3

Learners need to understand:

- The characteristics of an effective credit control system

- Organisational policies and procedures specific to the management of debts.

3.2   **Manage accounts receivables**   2, 3

Learners need to be able to:

- Prepare an aged receivables analysis report

- Apply the 80/20 rule to receivables balances

- Analyse ledger balances and take corrective action

- Calculate irrecoverable and doubtful debts:

  - Write offs and provisions

  - The impact on cash flow

  - VAT implications.

Chapter

3.3   Techniques to manage liquidity   3

Learners need understand:

- The effect of discounts on liquidity and cash flow

- The effect of changes to credit terms on liquidity and cash flow

- Options available to manage cash flow:

    - Invoice discounting

    - Factoring

    - Credit insurance.

Learners need to be able to:

- Calculate the effect of discounts on liquidity and cash flow

- Calculate the annual equivalent cost using simple or compound interest

- Calculate the impact on liquidity of:

    - Invoice discounting

    - Factoring

    - Credit insurance.

3.4   Communicate with stakeholders using a professional and ethical approach   2, 3, 4

Learners need to:

- Understand organisational policies when communicating with stakeholders

- Be able to communicate objectively to relevant stakeholders.

4   Understand different techniques available to collect debts

4.1   Legal and administrative procedures for debt collection   1, 4

Learners need to understand:

- The internal procedures used in the debt collection process

- The retention of title clause (basic and all monies)

Chapter

- The conditions required for retention of title claims to be effective

- The role of debt collection agencies and solicitors

- The use of small claims track, fast track and multi-track court processes

- Garnishee orders, warrants of execution and delivery

- Attachment of earnings and charging orders.

4.2	**Insolvency**	4

Learners need to understand:

- Advantages and disadvantages of initiating:

  - Liquidation, compulsory and voluntary

  - Receivership

  - Administration

  - Individual bankruptcy

  - Company Voluntary Arrangement (CVA)

- Processes to follow in the event of initiating:

  - Liquidation

  - Receivership

  - Administration

  - Individual bankruptcy

  - CVA.

Delivering this unit

Links with other units

This unit links with:

- Level 4 Cash and Financial Management

- Level 4 Drafting and Interpreting Financial Statements.

THE ASSESSMENT

Assessment type	Marking type	Duration of exam
Computer based assessment	Partially computer/ partially human marked	2 hours

Learning outcomes		Weighting
1	Understand relevant legislation and contract law that impacts the credit control environment.	15%
2	Understand how information is used to assess credit risk and grant credit in compliance with organisational policies and procedures.	45%
3	Understand the organisation's credit control processes for managing and collecting debts.	25%
4	Understand different techniques available to collect debts.	15%
Total		100%

STUDY SKILLS

Preparing to study

Devise a study plan

Determine which times of the week you will study.

Split these times into sessions of at least one hour for study of new material. Any shorter periods could be used for revision or practice.

Put the times you plan to study onto a study plan for the weeks from now until the assessment and set yourself targets for each period of study – in your sessions make sure you cover the whole course, activities and the associated questions in the workbook at the back of the manual.

If you are studying more than one unit at a time, try to vary your subjects as this can help to keep you interested and see subjects as part of wider knowledge.

When working through your course, compare your progress with your plan and, if necessary, re-plan your work (perhaps including extra sessions) or, if you are ahead, do some extra revision/practice questions.

Effective studying

Active reading

You are not expected to learn the text by rote, rather, you must understand what you are reading and be able to use it to pass the assessment and develop good practice.

A good technique is to use SQ3Rs – Survey, Question, Read, Recall, Review:

1   **Survey the chapter**

    Look at the headings and read the introduction, knowledge, skills and content, so as to get an overview of what the chapter deals with.

2   **Question**

    Whilst undertaking the survey ask yourself the questions you hope the chapter will answer for you.

3   Read

Read through the chapter thoroughly working through the activities and, at the end, making sure that you can meet the learning objectives highlighted on the first page.

4   Recall

At the end of each section and at the end of the chapter, try to recall the main ideas of the section/chapter without referring to the text. This is best done after short break of a couple of minutes after the reading stage.

5   Review

Check that your recall notes are correct.

You may also find it helpful to re-read the chapter to try and see the topic(s) it deals with as a whole.

Note taking

Taking notes is a useful way of learning, but do not simply copy out the text.

The notes must:

- be in your own words
- be concise
- cover the key points
- well organised
- be modified as you study further chapters in this text or in related ones.

Trying to summarise a chapter without referring to the text can be a useful way of determining which areas you know and which you don't.

Three ways of taking notes

1   Summarise the key points of a chapter

2   Make linear notes

A list of headings, subdivided with sub-headings listing the key points.

If you use linear notes, you can use different colours to highlight key points and keep topic areas together.

Use plenty of space to make your notes easy to use.

3   Try a diagrammatic form

The most common of which is a mind map.

To make a mind map, put the main heading in the centre of the paper and put a circle around it.

Draw lines radiating from this to the main sub-headings which again have circles around them.

Continue the process from the sub-headings to sub-sub-headings.

Highlighting and underlining

You may find it useful to underline or highlight key points in your study text – but do be selective.

You may also wish to make notes in the margins.

Revision phase

Kaplan has produced material specifically designed for your final examination preparation for this unit.

These include pocket revision notes and a bank of revision questions specifically in the style of the current syllabus.

Further guidance on how to approach the final stage of your studies is given in these materials.

Further reading

In addition to this text, you should also read the 'Accounting Technician' magazine every month to keep abreast of any guidance from the examiners.

Legislation

1

Introduction

This chapter covers the legislation that affects granting credit to customers, the characteristics of a contract, remedies for breaches of contract and other relevant legislation.

ASSESSMENT CRITERIA

Statute and contract law applicable to credit control (1.1)

Breach of contract and the circumstances in which they can be used effectively (1.2)

Terms and conditions associated with customer contracts (1.3)

Data protection and ethical considerations associated with credit control activities (1.4)

Legal and administrative procedures for debt collection (4.1)

CONTENTS

1 Contract law

2 Terms and conditions of contracts

3 Remedies for breach of contract

4 Data Protection Act

5 Other legislation

1 Contract law

1.1 Introduction

A sale or purchase is a legal contract between (usually) two parties. If credit is granted and then the invoice is not paid this is normally a breach of contract, hence the need for an awareness of contract law.

Control of the credit given to a customer is important for any organisation. Most organisations therefore appoint a **credit controller** whose responsibility it is to give appropriate credit terms to customers and ensure these terms are kept.

Receivables are an important part of **working capital** and **careful management** of this asset is required to maintain the company's **liquidity**.

Credit controllers do not need to be qualified lawyers but it is important to understand the legal background to contracts and credit arrangements.

1.2 Nature of a contract

The sale of goods and services is a type of contract and therefore the credit controller must ensure that each party abides by this contract.

 Definition

A **contract** is a legally binding agreement between two parties.

The **offeror** is the party making the offer (usually the buyer).

The **offeree** is the party accepting the offer (usually the seller).

The **law of contract** is the branch of the civil law that determines whether or not a promise is legally binding (i.e. enforceable by a court of law).

KAPLAN PUBLISHING

1.3   The essential characteristics of a contract

There are certain requirements if a contract is to be valid:

- **offer** and **acceptance** (i.e. an agreement)

- the **intention to create legal relations** (i.e. the parties must be willing to submit to the authority of the law and be bound by their contracts)

- **consideration**, in that both parties must do, or promise to do, something as their side of the contract

- the parties must have the **capacity**, or ability, **to contract and submit** themselves to the authority of the law (children and mentally disordered people are restricted)

- the parties must genuinely **consent to the terms** of the contract in that they must not have been mistaken by the contract terms, or lied to in negotiations – there must be **certainty of terms**

- the contract itself must be both **legal** and **possible**

- **written formalities** may be observed in **some** situations.

The key factors are a basic understanding of offer, acceptance, intention, consideration and capacity which will be detailed below.

1.4   Offer and acceptance

It is important to distinguish between an **offer** and an **invitation to treat**.

Definition

An **offer** is a definite and unequivocal statement of willingness to be bound on specified terms without further negotiations.

If you make an 'offer' it means that you are stating that you are willing to be bound to a contract in its current form with no changes required.

An offer can be in any form – oral, written or by conduct. However, it is not effective until it has been communicated to the offeree. For example, if a reward is offered for the return of a lost item, it cannot be claimed by someone who did not know of the reward before they returned the item.

Definition

An **invitation to treat** is not an offer. An invitation to treat means an invitation to the other party to make an offer.

Examples of an **invitation to treat** are an advertisement, a price ticket, goods on display in a shop or a trade price list where a written order from a customer is then the **offer**.

Once an offer has been made the next stage is for the contract to be accepted.

 Definition

Acceptance is the unqualified and unconditional agreement to all the terms of the offer.

To be effective, the acceptance must be made while the offer is still in force; it must be **absolute**, **unqualified** and **communicated** to the offeror by word or action.

Offer and acceptance constitute agreement.

 Example

Sofia has a sign in her car stating 'For sale, £1,200'.

Benjamin sees the invitation to treat and offers £800 to Sofia.

Sofia does not accept but responds to Benjamin that the lowest she would accept is £1,000.

Benjamin accepts so long as the car has a valid MOT certificate.

This is still not an agreement as Benjamin's response has a criterion that must be met.

Once Sofia proves she has a valid MOT and Benjamin accepts this certificate there has been:

- an invitation to treat (sign in the car)
- an offer (to buy/sell the car) and
- acceptance (Benjamin approves of the certificate).

Therefore an agreement has been formed.

Termination of an offer

An offer can be terminated by:

- **Revocation** – an offer can be revoked by the offeror at any time before acceptance, even if the offeror has agreed to keep the offer open. The revocation must be communicated to the offeree, i.e. it must be brought to his, her or their actual notice. The revocation can be communicated by the offeror or a reliable third party. There are two exceptions to the above rules on revocation:

  - If the offeree pays the offeror to keep the offer open, any revocation will amount to a breach of that contract. The offeree could claim damages for the loss of the opportunity to accept the offer, although he, she or they could not accept the offer itself.

  - The offeror cannot revoke his, her or their offer once the offeree has begun to perform the acts which would amount to acceptance, for example if part payment has been made.

- **Rejection** – the offeree may reject the offer outright or may make a counter offer. A counter offer is an offer made in response to an offer. A request for further details does not constitute a counteroffer.

- **Lapse** – an offer will lapse on:

  - the death of the offeror (unless the offeree accepts in ignorance of the death)

  - the death of the offeree

  - after the expiry of a fixed time (if any) or after a reasonable time. What is a reasonable time may depend on the subject matter of the contract; if the goods are perishable the time for lapse will be very short.

Once an offer has been terminated, it cannot be accepted.

1.5   Consideration

Before a simple binding contract exists, both parties must have **agreed to provide something of value to the other**. The price which each has to pay is termed the consideration and converts the mere promises of the parties into bargains **enforceable by the courts**.

 Definition

Consideration can be defined as 'some right, interest, profit or benefit accruing to one party, or some forbearance, detriment, loss or responsibility given, suffered or undertaken by the other'.

Example

Sofia is selling her car and has agreed to sell it for £1,000 to Benjamin.

Sofia will be suffering the loss of her car but the benefit of gaining £1,000.

Benjamin will be suffering the loss of £1,000 but the benefit of gaining the car.

When deciding on what the consideration will be, the following should be observed:

- **Sufficient** – it must be of some value (an item or service), even if it is minimal value (**peppercorn**). The consideration is usually of monetary value. Another legal term used here is '**adequate**', this means fair price. Consideration does not need to be adequate, but needs to be **sufficient** to form a contract.

- **Legal** – i.e. not against the law.

- **Should not be a duty which exists currently** – for example 'I will pay you £50 for not breaking the speed limit'. The speed limit is a legal requirement and is therefore a duty that already exists.

Consideration must be **executory** or **executed**, but **not past**:

- **Executory** – a promise to do something in the future is given in exchange for another promise to be done in the future. (I will pay you £10 if you get an A grade in your exam).

- **Executed** – a promise is actually executed, in exchange for another promise to be executed in the future. (I will pay you £5 now for you to wash my car at the weekend).

 Example

If Zara promises to paint Ali's house, in return for Ali's promise to pay Zara £500, there is a valid contract between them, with both parties having obligations to perform in the future. The consideration is executory. Once Zara has painted Ali's house, she is said to have provided executed consideration for Ali's promise to pay her £500.

- **Past** – a promise has been given or executed before and independently of the other promise.

Example

Sofia offers to sell her car to Benjamin for £1,000. Benjamin agrees to pay £1,000 for Sofia's car. There has been offer and acceptance and consideration (the car and the £1,000) – a simple contract has been formed.

However if Sofia had given the car to Benjamin as a gift, then at a later date Benjamin felt like he owed Sofia something for the car so told her that he would give her £1,000 next week, this would not constitute a contract since Sofia had already given the car to Benjamin (past consideration). Therefore there would be no valid consideration from Sofia.

1.6 Intention to create legal relations

If an offer is accepted, then an agreement is created, but this agreement does not automatically become a contract. If one of the parties wishes to invoke the aid of the law in enforcing the terms of the agreement against the other party, he, she or they must show that there had been an intention by both parties that the agreement was to create legal relations.

There is a presumption in social or domestic agreements that legal relations are not intended. But in **commercial agreements**, it is generally **assumed that relations are intended** unless there is a clause in the agreement to the contrary.

1.7 Capacity

Each party must have the legal power to bind itself contractually. For example persons under the age of eighteen (minors) and persons of unsound mind or under the influence of alcohol have limitations on their power to contract.

Test your understanding 1

Which of the following are features of a simple contract:

(i) Offer

(ii) Consideration

(iii) Relations

(iv) Acceptance

(v) Invitation

(vi) Certainty of terms

(vii) Intention to create legal relations

A All of them

B (i), (ii), (iii), (v), (vi) only

C (i), (ii), (iii), (iv) only

D (i), (ii), (iv), (vi) and (vii)

 Test your understanding 2

Mohammad has a notice in his shop window saying that the books he has for sale are half price. This is an example of:

A Offer

B Acceptance

C Invitation to treat

D Consideration

 Test your understanding 3

Harper is ordering an Indian takeaway on the telephone and says she will pay when she picks up the order. Which of the following would constitute consideration?

A Placing the order

B Paying for the order

C Saying she will pay for the order

D Picking up the order

Test your understanding 4

José is the owner of a haberdashery and put a notice in the window of his shop advertising that all fabric has 20% off. This is:

A   A completed contract

B   An acceptance of an offer

C   A contractual offer

D   An invitation to treat

 Test your understanding 5

If you are shopping in a supermarket a contract is formed?

A   When you put your goods in the trolley

B   When you take items off the shelves

C   When the checkout assistant takes your goods

D   When you pay for the goods

 Test your understanding 6

Alice has asked Callum for a price to paint her bedroom. Callum has said he can do it for £300 and Alice has agreed. Nearing the end of the job Callum asks Alice for £50 more as he has underestimated the work.

Does Alice have to pay Callum the extra £50?

Yes/No?

 Test your understanding 7

Dominique orders a Chinese takeaway over the telephone and says she will pay on delivery. Which of the following would constitute consideration?

A   Handing over the money to the delivery driver

B   Promising to pay for the takeaway

C   Accepting delivery of the takeaway

D   Calling the Chinese takeaway

2 Terms and conditions of contracts

2.1 Types of contracts

A **void** contract is one that **cannot be enforced by law**. An agreement to carry out an illegal act or an agreement that is impossible to carry out are examples of void contracts.

A **voidable** contract is a valid contract that **can be nullified** (to make legally null and void) – one party is bound to a contract but the other party is not, so can withdraw from the contract. If this happens then the contract becomes void. A contract between an adult and a minor is an example of a voidable contract as the adult is bound by the contract but the minor is not as they are not of legal age.

An **unenforceable contract** is one that is **valid** (i.e. meets all the requirements previously defined) but **if one party withdraws** from the contract the **courts of law will not enforce** them to meet the requirements of the contract. An example of this would be if one party was under duress or had been blackmailed into entering into the contract.

A **frustrated contract** occurs if an unforeseen event either renders contractual obligations impossible, or radically changes the party's principal purpose for entering into the contract.

Frustrated contracts could occur in the following circumstances:

- An item or building essential to the contract is destroyed, through no fault of either party.

- A law is passed subsequent to the formation of the contract, which makes the contract illegal.

- A person or group under contract becomes unavailable through death, illness or unavailability (generally only applies for the performance of personal services and not for generic commercial services such as building work, which could be performed by numerous individuals).

An important limitation is that economic hardship, or a 'bad bargain', will not render a contract frustrated. For example if you agreed to pay a builder to do some work, which the builder completes, you must then pay the agreed price, even if you can no longer afford the agreed price.

Test your understanding 8

A void contract is a contract that:

A   Is valid

B   Can be enforced by the law

C   Can be nullified

D   Cannot be enforced by the law

2.2   Contractual terms

A statement, written or oral, made during the negotiations leading to a contract, may be a **term** of the contract or merely a **representation** inducing the contract.

A **representation** is something that is said by the offeror in order to persuade the offeree to enter into the contract. It may or may not become a term of that contract.

The distinction between terms and representations is important because, if a statement is untrue, the remedies available to the innocent party differ:

- if the representation becomes a term of the contract, the innocent party has remedies for breach of the term as well as for misrepresentation

- if, however, the representation does not become a term of the contract, the innocent party will have remedies only for misrepresentation which are based on equitable remedies.

2.3   Sources of terms

Terms may be **express** or **implied**.

Express terms are those specifically inserted into the contract by one or both of the parties. They must be clear for them to be enforceable.

Implied terms are not expressly included in the contract, but they are nevertheless still part of the contract. They may be implied by statute or by the courts.

Express terms will generally override implied terms. However, some statutory terms cannot be overridden by express agreement (for example, terms inserted by the Consumer Rights Act).

There are three types of terms:

- A **condition** – is an important term going to the root of the contract. Breach can result in damages or discharge or both. Discharge entitles the innocent party to reject the contract and claim damages.

- A **warranty** – is a less important term, which is incidental to the main purpose of the contract. Breach of warranty results in damages only.

- An **innominate** or indeterminate term – is neither a condition nor a warranty. The remedy depends on the effects of the breach:

  - if trivial then damages only i.e. term is treated as if it were a warranty.

  - if serious then damages, discharge or both i.e. term is treated as if it were a condition.

3 Remedies for breach of contract

3.1 Introduction

Legal action can be taken to enforce a contract or to act as a remedy if a contract is breached. There are different types of **breach of contract**:

- **Actual** breach – when one party refuses or fails to complete the contract by the due date.

- **Fundamental breach** – is a breach of contract where the offending party fails to complete a contractual term that was so fundamental (hence the name of the breach) to the contract that another party was prevented from fulfilling their own responsibilities.

  This type of breach is not a subtle one, and it often is grounds for the aggrieved party to cancel the contract entirely. It is sometimes known as a **repudiatory** breach.

- **Anticipatory** breach – when one party informs the other party prior to the due date that the contract will not be completed.

  Compensation can be sought as soon as the innocent party is aware of the breach. Anticipatory breach is often referred to as **renunciation**.

Anticipatory breach may be express or implied:

- **Express** anticipatory breach occurs where one of the parties declares, before the due date for performance, that they have no intention of carrying out their contractual obligations.

- **Implied** anticipatory breach occurs where one of the parties does something which makes subsequent performance of their contractual undertaking impossible.

This section examines the legal remedies that may be available to any injured party as a result of a breach of contract.

3.2 Damages

The innocent party can claim damages from the guilty party. He, she or they may recover **damages** for any loss suffered as a result of the breach by bringing an **action for damages** for breach of contract.

The objective of damages is to put the innocent person into the same financial position he, she or they would have been in if the contract had been completed correctly. The amount of damages awarded should compensate the innocent party but should not punish the guilty party.

If the breach consists of the other party's failure to pay a debt (i.e. the contractually agreed price or other remuneration due under the contract), the appropriate course for the injured party is to bring an action for the **agreed sum** to recover that amount, this is an **action for price**.

If one party has already performed part of his, her or their obligations and the other party then repudiates the contract the course of action would be the remedy of **Quantum Meruit.** Under this remedy, the value of the contractual work which has already been performed is measured.

3.3 Equitable remedies

If damages are not sufficient then equitable remedies, such as **specific performance, injunctions or rescission**, may be awarded.

Specific performance – This is a court order to force the guilty party to positively complete his, her or their contractual obligations.

Injunction – This is a court order to force the guilty party to perform a negative obligation i.e. to cease doing something or to remove something that is in breach of contract.

Rescission – Restores the parties to their exact pre-contractual position.

3.4 Retention of title

The seller can add to the contract that the **'goods remain the property of the seller until payment has been received'**. This is a **basic retention of title clause** and means that if there is non-payment that the seller retains the ownership of the goods. This is particularly useful if the receivable becomes insolvent as the seller maintains priority over the goods when monies are being paid.

For a retention of title claim to be successfully enforced:

- the goods need to be **clearly identifiable** (e.g. have a brand name or product number on them)

- the goods must not have been processed or improved in a manufacturing process.

Due to these requirements, the seller may insist that the goods are stored separately from similar goods belonging to other parties and clearly marked as coming from the seller.

 Test your understanding 9

The normal remedy for breach of contract due to non-payment of the debt is:

A   Action for remedy

B   Action for the goods

C   Action for specific performance

D   Action for price

 Test your understanding 10

Retention of title is:

A   The right of the seller to retain ownership of the goods until payment is made

B   The right of the purchaser to retain ownership of the goods received

C   The right of the purchaser to expect that title is retained by the seller even when payment has been received

D   The right of the seller to retain ownership of the goods until a cheque has been posted

Instead of the basic retention of title clause described above, a supplier could use an **'all monies' retention of title** clause instead. This reserves the title (ownership) of all goods supplied to the buyer until the buyer has settled all outstanding invoices from the seller. This avoids the needs to match specific goods at the buyer's premises with specific unpaid invoices.

✹ Test your understanding 11

Which of the following would be most helpful to the seller in a successful retention of title claim:

A   The goods are a standard product which are stored in the buyer's warehouse alongside similar products from a wide range of suppliers

B   The buyer operates a Just in Time system where purchased materials are swiftly used to produce a complex final product

C   The goods are perishable with a short shelf life

D   All goods are clearly marked with the brand name of the supplier

---

3.5 Late Payment of Commercial Debts (Interest) Act 1998

The late payment act allows businesses to **charge other business customers interest on overdue amounts** and allows businesses to cover late payments of bank borrowings. Interest can be charged:

- 30 days after the goods are supplied or the service is completed.
- 30 days after receipt of invoice (or the customer is told the amount due is payable).
- The agreed date for payment.

The interest rate is **8%** above the Bank of England base rate for the period the debt is late. The interest is based on the **VAT inclusive** amount and calculated as a simple interest rate.

It is also possible to charge a business a fixed sum for the cost of recovering a late commercial payment (sometimes called a **compensation entitlement**) on top of claiming interest from it.

The amount you are allowed to charge depends on the amount of debt:

Amount of debt (including VAT)	Charge
Up to £999.99	£40
£1,000 to £9,999.99	£70
£10,000 or more	£100

 Example

A debt of £3,000 exclusive of VAT has been outstanding for 60 days. The Bank of England base rate is 0.5%. The late payment charge is:

3,000 × 1.2 (VAT) × 0.085 (8% plus base rate) × 60/365 = £50.30

A compensation entitlement of £70 could also be claimed as the amount of the debt is between £1,000 and £9,999.99.

 Test your understanding 12

A debt of £9,000 (VAT exclusive) has been outstanding for 45 days. The Bank of England base rate is 0.7%.

How much is the combined late payment charge and compensation entitlement?

A   £166.53

B   £185.84

C   £206.52

D   £215.84

4 Data Protection Act

4.1 Introduction

Due to the growth in the use of computer technology the Data Protection Act 1998 was introduced to make **certain restrictions** on the use of data about **individuals** and the **use of personal data**. It is likely that your organisation will hold computer data about credit customers and therefore you need to be aware of the broad outlines of the Act. It was then updated in 2018 by the Data Protection Act 2018 and sits alongside General Data Protection Regulation (GDPR) regulations.

However, it is important to realise that the Act relates to data **held about individuals not about organisations** so will only be relevant to non-corporate customers or to data about individuals who belong to a customer organisation.

The Data Protection Act gives individuals the right to know what information is held about them. It provides a framework to ensure that personal information is handled properly.

The Act works in two ways.

- Firstly, it gives rules and principles concerning the use of data.

- Secondly, it provides individuals with important rights concerning data held about them.

There are, however, exemptions to the Data Protection Act. For example:

- Any personal data that is held by MI5 and MI6 for a national security reason is not covered.

- Personal data held for domestic purposes only at home does not have to keep to the rules – e.g. a list of your friends' addresses.

4.2 Definitions

Personal data is information held about an individual, not only factual information but also expressions of opinion about that individual.

Data users are individuals or organisations who use personal data.

A **computer bureau** is an individual or organisation which processes personal data for data users, or allows data users to process personal data on its equipment.

4.3 The key principles of the Act

- Data may only be used for the **specific purposes** for which it was collected.

- Data **must not be disclosed** to other parties without the consent of the individual whom it is about, unless there is legislation or other overriding legitimate reason to share the information (for example, the prevention or detection of crime). It is an offence for other parties to obtain this personal data without authorisation.

- **Individuals have a right of access to the information held about them,** subject to certain exceptions (for example, information held for the prevention or detection of crime).

- Personal information may be **kept for no longer than is necessary** and must be kept up to date.

- Personal information **may not be sent outside the European Economic Area** unless the individual whom it is about has consented or adequate protection is in place, for example, by the use of a prescribed form of contract to govern the transmission of the data.

- Subject to some exceptions for organisations that only do very simple processing, and for domestic use, all entities that process personal information must **register with the Information Commissioner's Office**.

- Entities holding personal information are required to have adequate **security measures in place**. Those include technical measures (such as firewalls) and organisational measures (such as staff training).

- Subjects have the right to have **factually incorrect information corrected** (note: this does not extend to matters of opinion).

- All data users and computer bureaux have to **register with the Data Protection Registrar** – the data user must then only hold data and use data for the purposes which are registered.

- Processing of personal data is forbidden except in the following circumstances:

    - with the consent of the individual

    - due to a legal obligation

    - due to a contractual obligation

    - due to a contractual arrangement

    - in the public interest

    - to protect the vital interests of the individual.

- If data is obtained from a third party the data subject must be given:

  - the identity of the controller of the data

  - the purposes for which the data is being processed

  - the data that will be disclosed and to whom.

- Data subjects have the right to a copy of the data held, the right to know why the data is being processed and the logic behind the processing. Data subjects may seek compensation through the courts for damage or distress caused by the loss, destruction, inaccuracy or unauthorised disclosure of personal data.

- Data subjects can apply to the courts or Registrar for inaccurate data to be corrected or removed from the data user's files.

- Individuals have the right to object to a system automated decision about them that has had no human involvement, and have that decision reviewed by a human.

 Test your understanding 13

The Data Protection Act applies to (pick as many as appropriate):

A   Data about individuals, companies and government departments

B   Data about individuals only

C   Data about companies only

D   Data about companies and individuals only

E   Only manual records

F   Only computer records

G   All records held by the company

H   Only records of opinions

As well as a legal duty, businesses also have an ethical duty to protect customers' (and employees') personal data. Any breach of the Data Protection Act and/or leak of personal data may have not only legal implications for the business but reputational ones too.

It is vital that businesses have controls in place to safeguard personal data (such as names, addresses, email addresses, credit card details, medical history etc.) and do not keep data any longer than required. If a data leak does occur then the people affected should be notified as soon as possible, and actions taken to limit the damage of the data leak and spread of the personal data.

5 Other legislation

5.1 Trade Descriptions Act

The Trade Descriptions Act states that manufacturers, retailers and the service industry must **correctly describe what they are selling**. It is a **criminal offence to make a false or misleading statement** about the goods or services being provided i.e. **misrepresented** in any way.

From May 2008, the **Consumer Protection from Unfair Trading Regulations 2008** replaced most of the Trade Descriptions Act 1968.

There are three main sections in the "Regulations". These are as follows:

- A general ban on unfair commercial practices. A commercial practice is 'unfair' if it fits both of the following requirements:

  1 It falls below the good-faith standards of skill and care that a trader in that industry would be expected to exercise towards customers.

  2 It affects, or is likely to affect, consumers' ability to make an informed decision about whether to purchase a particular product.

- A ban on misleading and aggressive practices which are assessed in light of the effect they have, or are likely to have, on the average consumer. A commercial practice is considered aggressive if, by means of harassment, coercion or undue influence, it significantly impairs (or is likely to significantly impair) the average consumer's freedom of choice or conduct, which then leads the consumer to take a decision that they would otherwise not have made.

- The 'blacklist' of commercial practices which will always be unfair and so are banned outright. There are a number of banned practices they include:

  1 Limited offers – falsely stating that a product will only be available for a very limited time.

  2 False free offers – describing a product as free or without charge if the consumer has to pay anything other than the unavoidable cost of responding to the offer and collecting or paying for delivery of the item.

  3 Pressure selling – creating the impression that the consumer cannot leave the premises until a contract is formed.

KAPLAN PUBLISHING

5.2 Unfair Contract Terms Act

Contracts must be written in **language that is understandable** and any part of the contract that acts more favourably for the vendor than the consumer is unfair and not binding.

This is the most important statute affecting exclusion clauses and is largely restricted to business liability i.e. liability arising during business or from occupation of premises for business purposes. It is not possible to exclude liability for death or personal injury and all other losses are subject to a test of reasonableness.

5.3 Consumer Rights Act 2015

The Consumer Rights Act **applies when the title of the goods has passed from the vendor to the buyer** and states that as a buyer you have three statutory rights:

1	Goods should be of **'satisfactory quality'**, they shouldn't be faulty or damaged when you receive them.

2	That the goods should be **fit for the purpose** they are supplied for.

3	Goods supplied must match any description given to you; they should be **'as described'**.

The rules also include digital content in this definition.

Under the Consumer Rights Act buyers are entitled to a full refund if faulty goods are returned within **30 days**.

If faulty goods are returned after 30 days then the seller has the opportunity to repair or replace the item(s) rather than a refund (under the **Refund – Repair – Replace** rule).

If faulty goods are returned **within 6 months** then it is presumed the fault existed at purchase (it will be up to the seller to prove otherwise), if goods are returned **after 6 months** then the seller may ask for proof that the fault existed at the time of purchase.

The Consumer Rights Act also covers providing services, for example work carried out by accountants, solicitors, builders. The Act means that all contracts for services must do the following:

•	The trader must perform the service with reasonable care and skill.

•	Information that is spoken or written is binding where the consumer relies on it.

•	Where the price is not agreed beforehand, the service must be provided for a reasonable price.

•	Unless a particular timescale for performing the service is set out or agreed, the service must be carried out in a reasonable time.

If the service does not satisfy these criteria, you are entitled to the following remedies:

- The trader should either redo the element that is inadequate, or perform the whole service again at no extra cost to you, within a reasonable time and without causing you significant inconvenience.

- If repeat performance is not possible, you can claim a price reduction. Depending on how severe the failings are, this could be up to 100% of the cost, and the trader should refund you within 14 days of agreeing that you're entitled to a refund.

5.4 Consumer Credit Act 1974 and 2006

The Consumer Credit Act 1974 and 2006 requires:

- Businesses that offer goods or services on credit or lend money to individuals to be **licensed** by the **Financial Conduct Authority (FCA)**. Trading without a licensing arrangement is a criminal offence and can result in a fine and/or imprisonment.

- That the borrower can settle a regulated consumer credit agreement early by giving notice to the lender and paying the amount due less a rebate. The borrower is also entitled to information about the amount needed to settle.

- The seller lays down rules requiring information to be given to borrowers or hirers before entry into a consumer credit or hire agreement.

- Stipulates 'cooling off' periods when a credit agreement has been entered into.

- Gives additional protection to buyers for **purchases between £100 and £30,000 made on a credit card**. If there is misrepresentation or a breach of contract by a seller and no resolution can be obtained, a claim can be made against the credit card company instead.

Test your understanding 14

Calvin is sold some lime cordial by Hobbs but when Calvin opens the bottle it is actually lemonade. Calvin can claim for breach of contract due to:

A   Fiduciary misconduct

B   Misrepresentation

C   Misuse of Sales Act

D   Unfair Contract Terms Act

5.5 Professional ethics in the context of credit control

Finance professionals can help in creating and promoting an ethics-based culture that discourages unethical or illegal practices, including money laundering, terrorist financing, fraud, theft, bribery, non-compliance with applicable regulations, bullying and short-term decision-making.

Having a better awareness of the relevant legislation will help safeguard businesses from breaking the law, and also help the business maintain a good reputation with customers and suppliers.

 # 6 Summary

This chapter has covered the legislation that affects granting credit to customers, the characteristics of a contract, remedies for breaches of contract and other relevant legislation.

The sale of goods on credit to a customer is a contract and therefore you need to be aware of the legal background in terms of the general nature of contract law. You must also be aware of the basic provisions of the Data Protection Act and other legal terms and conditions in relation to a contract.

Test your understanding answers

 ### Test your understanding 1

Answer D

 ### Test your understanding 2

Answer C – An advert in a shop is nearly always an invitation to treat.

 ### Test your understanding 3

Answer C – The promise to pay is an executory consideration.

 ### Test your understanding 4

Answer D – An advert in a shop is nearly always an invitation to treat.

 ### Test your understanding 5

Answer C – You taking the goods to the checkout is effectively your offer to buy them and the shop assistant taking them is acceptance.

 ### Test your understanding 6

No – the additional amount does not have to be paid as the agreement was for £300.

Test your understanding 7

Answer B – The promise to pay is an executory consideration.

 Test your understanding 8

Answer D

 Test your understanding 9

Answer D – An action for price is an order to pay the debt owed.

 Test your understanding 10

Answer A

 Test your understanding 11

Answer D

If the goods are clearly marked with the supplier's brand name it will make them easier to identify if the goods need to be reclaimed.

If the goods are standard and mixed in with goods from other suppliers (answer A) they will be impossible to identify. If the goods are swiftly used in the buyer's manufacturing process (answer B) then a retention of title claim will be unsuccessful. If the goods are perishable (answer C) then any reclaimed goods are likely to be worthless.

Test your understanding 12

Answer D – £215.84

Vat inclusive amount of the debt = £9,000 × 1.2 = £10,800

Late payment interest = £10,800 × 45/365 × 0.087 (8% + 0.7%) = £115.84

Compensation is £100 since the VAT inclusive amount is over £10,000, hence the combined amount is £115.84 + £100 = £215.84

 Test your understanding 13

Answers B and G

 Test your understanding 14

Answer B – The contents of the bottle had been misrepresented (it was not what was advertised on the label).

Granting credit

Introduction

In this chapter we look at why a business grants credit and what information is required to decide whether to grant credit or extend credit terms and conditions.

ASSESSMENT CRITERIA	CONTENTS
Sources of credit status and assessment methods used in granting credit (2.1)	1 Granting credit
	2 External sources of information
Credit status of existing and potential customers using relevant ratios and performance indicators (2.2)	3 Internal sources of information
	4 Analysis of accounts
Reasons for granting, refusing, amending or extending credit (2.3)	5 Liquidity ratios
Methods for the management of debts (3.1)	6 Profitability ratios
	7 Debt ratios
Manage accounts receivables (3.2)	8 Example and activities
Communicate with stakeholders using a professional and ethical approach (3.4)	9 Overtrading
	10 Credit terms and conditions
	11 Refusal of credit

1 Granting credit

1.1 Introduction

Payment for goods can be made either by cash or on credit. Payment by **cash** (including cheque, credit/debit cards) means that the business received what it is owed for the goods or services at the time they are provided. Payment on **credit** where an invoice is raised means that the business provides the goods or service and payment is received later. This creates trade receivables for the business – customers who owe the business money.

1.2 The trade receivable balancing act

Trade receivables form part of the **working capital cycle** and as such, management of trade receivables is very important in **maintaining the liquidity** of the company.

For many businesses their entire turnover is made on credit terms with very few business-to-business transactions being made for cash and likewise fewer business-to-customer transactions are in cash.

Trade receivable management principles involve a series of balancing acts. The following diagram should be remembered.

Balancing costs and benefits of trade receivables

Benefit of granting trade credit	Costs of granting trade credit
– Attractive to customers	– Finance costs
– Marketing benefits	– Irrecoverable debts costs
	– Administration costs

The main benefit to the company is that **customers like to be given trade credit**, rather than paying on delivery of goods. Thus, generous credit terms often have a beneficial impact on sales.

Giving a customer credit terms for payment is always a risk and all companies try to reduce this risk and potential irrecoverable debt problems.

Test your understanding 1

Which of the following is not a reason for companies to offer credit terms to their customers?

A   To reduce expenses

B   To increase sales

C   To help grow the business

D   To improve customer relations

1.3   Credit control

The following need to be in place to reduce the risks associated with granting credit:

- The **credit manager** ensures appropriate credit terms are negotiated with customers and are then adhered to. The manager usually reports to the finance director or financial controller; sometimes, however, he/she/they may be found within the sales or marketing department.

- A company policy – the credit manager needs to ascertain the basis of the **company's credit terms**. This may have been decided upon by the finance director or has to be developed by the credit controller in consultation with his/her/their superior and the sales department. This has the advantage of allowing a flexible method to develop which can cater for differing situations.

- Consideration needs to be given to the **nature of the market** and any **seasonal fluctuations**, the expected level of sales, the marketing strategy and the policies of competitors.

- It must be clear who **establishes the credit terms**: the sales manager or the credit manager, or both in consultation – in which case, their joint policy must be clearly documented to avoid any misunderstandings. The credit manager also needs to establish whether he/she/they has the authority to accept or reject new customers or new orders.

- The correct **evaluation of credit risk** is the most difficult and the most vital part of the credit manager's role. It is not only new accounts that need to be considered, the credit manager needs constantly to **review his/her/their established customer base** to ensure that they continue to be a safe risk and have not slipped with their payments.

There are various ways of obtaining information about customers both from one's own experience and from internal and external sources and references. All available information needs to be collected and assimilated so that appropriate credit terms can be given to the customer.

Once agreed, these terms will then form the basis of the contract of sale between the two parties and trading can proceed smoothly.

1.4 Ethical issues with granting credit

A credit controller must demonstrate objectivity when deciding whether to offer credit to a company.

 Definition – Objectivity

Objectivity means that a person must not allow bias, conflict of interest or undue influence of others to override professional or business judgements.

There are a number of ways in which a credit controller's objectivity could be threatened. These include:

- **The self-interest threat** – a credit controller may be able to gain financially (or otherwise) if a request for credit is accepted. This could arise, for example, from a direct or indirect interest in the organisation or from fear of losing the business or having his, her or their employment terminated or because of undue commercial pressure from within or outside the firm.

- **The self-review threat** – there will be a threat to objectivity if a decision to offer or decline credit made by the credit controller needs to be challenged or re-evaluated by him or her in the future.

- **The advocacy threat** – there is a threat to a credit controller's objectivity if he, she or they becomes a supporter for or against the position taken by the organisation. The degree to which this presents a threat to objectivity will depend on the individual circumstances.

- **The familiarity or trust threat** – the credit controller may be influenced by his, her or their knowledge of the organisation, or may have a relationship with a member of staff at the organisation, which could lead to the credit controller becoming too trusting.

- **The intimidation threat** – the possibility that the credit controller may become intimidated by pressures, actual or feared, applied by the organisation or employer or by another party.

Where a credit controller decides to accept a request for credit or increase a credit limit where any significant threat to objectivity has been identified, they should be able to demonstrate that they have considered the availability and effectiveness of safeguards and have reasonably concluded that those safeguards will adequately preserve their objectivity.

 Example

You are the credit controller and a company is asking for credit that:

- you own shares in – this could be viewed as a conflict of interest

- you receive excessive hospitality and discounts from – this could be seen as an attempt to influence (bribe?) you and compromise your objectivity.

2 External sources of information

2.1 Trade credit references

Traditionally, creditworthiness has been checked by asking the customer to supply trade references from **two other suppliers**. As it can be assumed that customers will not quote suppliers likely to give a bad report, it is **unwise to rely on this procedure alone**. Beware of organisations that pay their two referee suppliers promptly, but pay all other suppliers late. Used in conjunction with other information, this procedure however may be helpful.

Trade reference requests should be made **formally** and should ask for credit terms. Often a standard form can be used requesting:

- the exact name of the potential customer

- the usual credit terms offered

- the expected level of business

- names and addresses of two trade referees.

From this information, the credit manager can contact the trade referees and ensure the potential customer can pay on time and adhere to agreed credit terms.

Example

John James Ltd
4 The Parade
York YK4 6TP

PRIVATE AND CONFIDENTIAL
Credit Controller
Priory Trading
44 Kiln Terrace
York YK3 4XS   10 May 20X2

Dear Sir or Madam

We recently received a request from Donald & Sons, a customer of ours, who gave yourselves as a reference. I would be grateful if you could assist us by answering the following questions and returning them in the stamped addressed envelope provided.

1   How long have Donald & Sons been trading with you?

     2 years   months

2   When Donald & Sons opened an account with you, did the company supply you with suitable trade and credit references?

     YES / (NO)

3   What are your normal credit terms for Donald & Sons?

     Amount: £10,000

     Terms: Cash   Weekly   (Monthly)   Other

4   Does Donald & Sons make payments in accordance with your terms?

     (YES) / NO / SLOW PAYER

5   Have you ever had to suspend credit facilities to Donald & Sons?

     YES / (NO)

     If Yes, when?

6   Please supply any other information that you consider relevant.

Thank you for your help.

Yours faithfully

B Down

B Down
Brian Down Credit Controller Solution

2.2 Bank references

It is usual to take up bank references at the same time as trade references. Requests to the bank need to be **precise**; detailing the **amount of credit** you envisage giving the customer and the **credit period**.

Bank replies are usually structured in one of three ways:

(1) an **unqualified**, **positive** assurance

(2) a **general indication** that the firm is operating normally

(3) a **guarded statement**, indicating that 'capital is fully employed' or 'we are unable to speak for your figures'.

 Example

Northern Bank plc

Doncaster Branch
501 High Street
Doncaster DN3 4XL

Credit Controller
John James Ltd
4 The Parade
York YK4 6TP

19 May 20X2

Dear Sir or Madam

Reference: Donald & Sons

I refer to your letter dated 10 May 20X2 enquiring about the creditworthiness of the above. In our view, Donald & Sons is reasonably constituted and should prove good for your figures.

Yours faithfully

G Donarski

Gerald Donarski
Manager

Test your understanding 2

When taking up bank references they usually provide one of three types of references. Which of the following is not a standard bank reference?

A   Unqualified, positive

B   Qualified, positive

C   Guarded

D   General indication

2.3   Credit reference agency reports

Credit agencies are not covered by the Data Protection Act but by the Consumer Credit Act 1974 and 2006 which actually gives stronger protection in terms of the handling of information.

One of the most widely used registers is that of Dun & Bradstreet. It summarises data for over 256 million businesses in over 200 countries, including the **name, address, date of formation, nominal and issued share capital, existing mortgages and charges, proprietors and associates, credit rating** and Dun & Bradstreet rating.

The vital piece of information for the credit manager is the **credit rating** which indicates the **average amount of credit given to the firm**. This helps the credit manager to assess the relative size of the proposed credit limit to the potential customer.

The usefulness of a report from an agency depends on the skill and competence of the agency. A specialised agency for the particular industry concerned can normally offer more detached information, but the credit manager needs to research the agency carefully.

The questions of cost and speed of reporting should not be considered as agencies who offer low-cost reports are immediately suspect. Worthwhile reports cannot be produced cheaply and, although speed is important, it is very difficult to specify minimum reporting periods for gathering information from so many different sources.

The credit manager should look for the following **contents** in the report on the potential customer:

- name and address; associated companies with names and addresses

- name of proprietors, partners and/or directors

- amount of authorised and issued share capital

- description of the customer's activities

- latest statement of financial position and statement of profit or loss

- a list of secured charges and mortgages

- name and address of its financial advisers, bankers

- payment pattern/experience from other suppliers

- a recommended credit limit based on the findings in the report.

The **problems** with agency reports are as follows:

- **New companies have no track record**. It is therefore very difficult to form a judgement.

- It takes time for current information to be analysed and fed into computer/appraisal systems. It is possible for very relevant information (such as the collapse of a major customer) not to be in a report.

- Suppliers' references may be too old to be of value.

2.4 Statutory accounts

Historical financial information can provide information on the financial position of a business – the levels of profitability and liquidity it has maintained in the previous years.

It may also be possible to access the management accounts of a business if they are provided by the customer. This is particularly useful with new companies or those who are unaudited.

2.5 Credit circle reports

A credit circle is a **group of people** with a common interest for example a trade association. These people meet on a regular basis to **share information on credit related matters**, such as late payers or bad trade receivables.

This information is both useful for current credit customers – are the customers struggling to pay other debts? – and potential credit customers – what is their/has their credit management been like?

2.6 Official publications

The press provide an **up-to-date commentary** on the situation within local and national companies. If the proposed customer is a big national company, reading The Financial Times enables the credit manager to keep up-to-date with half-yearly reports, comments on the customer as well as keeping abreast of industry trends and problems. Smaller more local companies are commented upon in regional and local papers.

Often produced weekly or monthly, **trade journals** are another valuable source of information and **commentary on trends and results**.

3 Internal sources of information

3.1 Introduction

Internal sources of information are particularly useful when assessing current customers if, for example, they wish to change their credit limit.

Internal sources can include conversations, emails and minutes of staff meetings.

3.2 The sales ledger

A company's sales ledger, where each sale is recorded and all payments from customers are noted, will be one of the main internal sources of information.

The sales ledger will provide the basis for investigation of:

- Trading history of existing credit customers – can be a very useful tool when deciding to extend credit terms or limits. It can show how long a company has been in operation and how well trading has been going.

- Aged receivables analysis – The aged analysis of trade receivables analyses the **balance due** from each trade receivable according to the amount of time that each individual invoice has been outstanding.

- Irrecoverable debts – An **irrecoverable debt** is a debt which the credit manager is fairly certain will never be received from the customer.

Effective monitoring of trade receivable balances can only occur if the accounts information is correct.

3.3 Sales representatives' knowledge

A company's sales staff will have **first hand information** on existing customers and may have met or known of potential customers, all of which is useful to the credit manager.

It is beneficial to the credit manager to train the sales staff to observe and listen for information on customers' ability to pay by finding out:

- the level of activity of the business

- the impression/competence of the customer's staff and premises

- the names of other suppliers

- future plans of the customer/client

- any other information possible.

This provides more **background information to analyse** alongside other facts, though the credit manager would need to be mindful of the sales representatives' main aim to increase sales.

3.4 Analysis of accounts

One of the most useful sources of external information are the **annual accounts** of the customer (if it is a company). From these, various statistics can be calculated **internally** to help to analyse the company's situation.

However, it must be remembered that the financial accounts only give **historic data** and it is often the case that the most recent accounts available from companies are at least 12 months out of date.

Whatever accounts are produced for examination, it is necessary to **respect the confidential nature** of the documents and the credit manager must exercise due care in this regard.

The calculations for this are looked at in more detail later in this chapter.

Test your understanding 3

In gathering credit information on a potential client you would use both internal sources of credit information and external sources of credit information. Which of the following is an example of internal information?

A   Trade references

B   Sales representatives' knowledge

C   Credit agency

D   Bank references

Test your understanding 4

Which of the following is not a method of analysing credit control information?

A   Aged trade payable analysis

B   Credit circles

C   Key performance indicators

D   Trading history

3.5 How to use the information

There are various sources of information that can be used to analyse trade receivables.

When analysing current credit customers you may need to decide on which customers to focus the debt collection efforts on.

When deciding whether or not to grant credit to a customer you will need to be able to analyse any information gathered.

Some of the techniques mentioned are more useful for current credit customers, some for potential credit customers and some are useful for analysing both:

Current credit customers	Potential credit customers	Current and potential credit customers
Aged trade receivable analysis	Trade references	Credit circle reports
Sales ledger information	Bank references	Performance indicators
		Trading history
		Credit rating agencies
		Press reports
		Trade journals
		Status reports
		Sale representatives knowledge

Test your understanding 5

Which of the following information should be used to assess the credit status of a new customer?

(i)   Aged trade receivable analysis

(ii)   Draft contract for trade

(iii) Trade references

(iv) Bank references

(v)   Financial accounts

(vi) Copies of outstanding invoices

A   All of the above

B   (iii) only

C   (iii), (iv) and (v) only

D   (ii) and (v) only

 Test your understanding 6

Which of the following would usually be used to assess the credit status of a current customer?

(i)   Aged trade receivable analysis

(ii)   Draft contract for trade

(iii) Trade references

(iv) Bank references

(v)   Financial accounts

(vi) Copies of outstanding invoices

A   (i) only

B   (i), (v) and (vi) only

C   (v) and (vi) only

D   All of the above

4 Analysis of accounts

4.1 Key performance indicators

Key performance indicators can be calculated to analyse financial accounts provided by a business. There are four aspects of a company's performance that the credit manager should consider:

- **Liquidity** – the ability of the company to pay its debts from its current assets, i.e. there are sufficient liquid resources.

- **Profitability** – this is obviously important as, in the long run, an unprofitable company will not survive.

- **Debt** – this is concerned with risk. How much capital (equity) is there compared to debt (loans).

- **Cash flow** – what is the cash position of the potential customer? Is it improving or worsening?

This information can be used to decide on whether to **offer credit terms** to a new company or whether to **extend credit terms** to a current credit customer. With current credit customers it is also a useful tool to be able to **assess how the business is progressing** – have ratios improved or worsened. This could lead to a **change in credit policy** being implemented.

Before examining the various accounting ratios in detail, it is important to remember that:

(a) an opinion cannot be formed from one year's statistics alone – it is more useful to develop trends for several years/months before concluding

(b) it is helpful to be able to compare the company's statistics with other companies in the same industrial sector – hopefully the company concerned will be better than average

(c) the accounts may be distorted due to inter-company transactions, group funding etc. and so an opinion can only be formed by looking at the accounts for the whole group

(d) statistics are only statistics! It is very easy in recessionary or inflationary times for the position of a company to change very quickly from profitable to loss making, so the credit manager must not become blinded by numbers alone.

The next few sections work through each of the assessable areas of a business and provides the calculations that can be used.

5 Liquidity ratios

5.1 Current ratio

This is a common method of analysing working capital and is generally accepted as the measure of **short-term liquidity**. It indicates the extent to which the current liabilities of a business are covered by the current assets.

$$\text{Current ratio} = \frac{\text{Current assets}}{\text{Current liabilities}}$$

The aim is to ensure that current liabilities can be met as they fall due. Sometimes it is suggested that if the current ratio is below a certain level (which is usually given as between 1.5 and 2), the business should become seriously concerned.

This should not always be taken to be a strict rule, because:

(a) current liabilities include the bank overdraft which, in practice, is not repayable within one year (technically, of course, repayable on demand)

(b) different types of industry will have different typical current ratios. For example a supermarket will have high payable levels and high inventories but very few trade receivables; whereas a manufacturing business will not only have high payable and inventory levels but also significant levels of trade receivables.

Even considering the points above a current ratio of below 1:1 would be of concern to any business as it indicates that there are insufficient current assets to cover the current liabilities as they fall due.

This ratio will change due to any movements in working capital (e.g. paying suppliers early, offering an early settlement discount, taking out a loan to boost cash levels).

5.2 Quick ratio

The quick ratio is also known as the **acid test ratio**. It is calculated in the same way as for the current ratio but inventories are excluded from current assets.

$$\text{Quick ratio} = \frac{\text{Current assets} - \text{Inventory}}{\text{Current liabilities}}$$

This ratio is a much better test of the **immediate liquidity** of a business because inventory is assumed to be the least liquid of the current assets due to the length of time necessary to convert it into cash (via sales and trade receivables).

Although increasing liquid resources more usually indicate favourable trading, it could be that funds are not being used to their best advantage (e.g. a large unused cash balance).

As with the current ratio, a quick ratio of less than 1:1 would be of concern to a business.

5.3 Trade receivables collection period

$$\text{Trade receivables collection period (days)} = \frac{\text{Trade receivables}}{\text{(Credit) Sales revenue}} \times 365$$

If a **credit sales** figure is provided then this is a more accurate figure to use in the calculation of the accounts receivable collection period, if credit sales are not provided then total sales should be used.

This indicates the average length of time it takes the company **to receive the cash from its credit customers**. This is not directly relevant to the decision whether or not to grant credit but it can give useful information about how the company's credit control department operates.

The average collection period will be influenced by the credit terms offered, any early settlements offered and by the effectiveness of the credit control department.

NOTE

In financial accounting revenue in the statement of profit or loss is shown net of VAT; the receivables figure in the statement of financial position includes VAT as this represents the total amount due. Generally we do not know how much this amount of VAT might be as this could be made up of exempt, zero or standard rated supplies.

Therefore, for general calculation of receivables days from financial statements we have to use the figures provided. It would be more accurate to use VAT inclusive amounts for sales and receivables.

If the figures are specific to a particular receivable and the VAT position is clear, the sales figure should include VAT as the receivables amount also includes VAT. This is also applicable to payables and purchases.

KAPLAN PUBLISHING

5.4 Trade payables payment period

$$\text{Trade payables payment period (days)} = \frac{\text{Trade payables}}{\text{Cost of sales}} \times 365$$

If a **credit purchases** figure is provided then this is a more accurate figure to use in the calculation of the trade payables payment period. However if no purchases figure is provided then **cost of sales** should be used instead (this is the more common scenario).

This ratio is **directly relevant** to the decision whether or not to grant credit as it indicates the average length of time a company takes to **pay its current credit suppliers**.

It is desirable for the trade receivables' collection period to be shorter than the trade payables' payment period. This way the company collects what is due before it has to pay out to its own trade payables.

The payment period will be influenced by the credit terms (and any early settlement discounts) offered to the company, as well as their promptness and ability to pay invoices on time.

5.5 Inventory holding period

This ratio indicates whether a business's inventories are justified in relation to its sales. It estimates how long inventory is held in the business before it is sold.

$$\text{Inventory holding period (days)} = \frac{\text{Inventory}}{\text{Cost of sales}} \times 365$$

If the inventory holding period increases this may indicate excess inventories or sluggish sales.

The average holding period will be influenced by the nature of the goods (perishable goods will have a shorter holding period), the nature of production (a Just-In-Time system would have a very low inventory holding period, a company who bulk buys materials will have a longer holding period) and the company's stock control policy.

5.6 Working capital cycle

 Definition

Working capital is the short-term net assets of the business made up of inventory, receivables, payables and cash.

Working capital is the capital available for conducting the day to day operations of an organisation. It is normally expressed as the excess of current assets over current liabilities.

Working capital management is the management of all aspects of both current assets and current liabilities, to minimise the risk of insolvency whilst maximising the return on assets.

The **working capital cycle** or the **cash operating cycle** is the length of time between the company's outlay on raw materials, wages and other expenditures and the inflow of cash from the sale of goods. The faster a firm can 'push' items around the cycle the lower its investment in working capital will be.

Working capital is an investment which affects cash flows:

- When inventory is purchased, cash is paid to acquire it.

- Receivables represent the cost of selling goods or services to customers, including the costs of materials and the labour incurred.

- The cash tied up in working capital is reduced to the extent that inventory is finance by trade payables. If suppliers give a firm time to pay, the firm's cash flows are improved and working capital is reduced.

The working capital cycle (cash operating cycle) is calculated as:

Inventory holding period + Receivable collection period – Payables payment period

The working capital cycle:

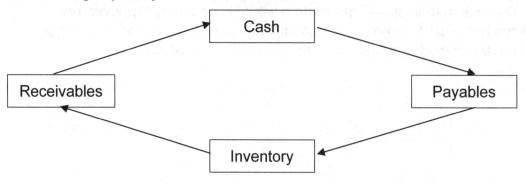

Time line:

Purchases   Sales Receipts from receivables

	Inventory days		Receivable days

Payable days	working capital cycle

Pay payables

The length of the cycle depends on:

*   how the balancing act between liquidity and profitability is resolved

*   the efficiency of management

*   the nature of the industry.

The optimum level is the amount that results in no idle cash or unused inventory, but that does not put a strain on liquid resources. Trying to shorten the cash cycle may have detrimental effects elsewhere, with the organisation lacking the cash to meet its commitments and losing sales since customers will generally prefer to buy from suppliers who are prepared to extend trade credit, and who have items available when required.

Additionally, any assessment of the acceptability or otherwise of the length of the cycle must take into account the nature of the business involved. A supermarket chain will tend to have a very low or negative cycle – they have very few, if any, credit customers, they have a high inventory turnover and they can negotiate quite long credit periods with their suppliers.

6 Profitability ratios

6.1 Gross profit margin

This ratio isolates the pure 'nuts and bolts' of a business, i.e. the sales revenue and what it costs to make those sales.

$$\text{Gross profit margin (\%)} = \frac{\text{Gross profit}}{\text{Sales revenue}} \times 100$$

The gross margin focuses on the trading activity of a business as it is the gross profit (revenue less cost of sales) as a percentage of revenue.

A high gross margin is desirable. It indicates that either sales prices and/ or volumes are high or that production costs are being kept well under control.

6.2   Operating profit margin

This ratio includes the other costs incurred in running a business.

$$\text{Operating profit margin (\%)} = \frac{\text{Operating profit}}{\text{Sales revenue}} \times 100$$

A high margin is desirable. It indicates that either sales prices and/or volumes are high or that **ALL** costs are being kept well under control.

6.3   Return on capital employed

Capital employed is normally measured as **equity plus non-current liabilities** (or, alternatively, **non-current assets plus current assets minus current liabilities**); it represents the long-term investment in the business.

Return on capital employed is frequently regarded as the **best measure** of profitability, indicating how successful a business is in utilising its assets.

This ratio is only meaningful when the true values of assets are known and used in the formula.

$$\text{Return on capital employed} = \frac{\text{Operating profit}}{\text{Capital employed}} \times 100$$

Operating profit is also called profit from operations.

A low return on capital employed is caused by either a low profit margin or a low asset turnover or both.   The aim is to see how effectively the business is using the money invested in it.

Care should be taken with the interpretation of this ratio for the following reasons:

*   It is based upon the statement of financial position values of the net assets rather than the true market value i.e. depreciation has been charged against the cost of the assets.

*   A high ROCE may be solely due to accounting for depreciation reducing the capital employed figure rather than a high profit figure.

*   As the statement of financial position values are based upon historical cost then the age structure of the assets of the business can also affect the return on capital employed.

- Often new investment does not bring immediate profits. This may be for a number of reasons. It may take time for the organisation's employees to learn how to use the new equipment. Alternatively it may take the organisation time to obtain enough orders to use the new facilities to the full. (This may result in a temporary reduction in the ROCE).

6.4 Interest cover

This provides the ratio of profit before interest and tax (PBIT), to the interest charged on loans or the Finance cost.

$$\text{Interest cover} = \frac{\text{Profit before interest and tax}}{\text{Finance cost}}$$

Note: Profit before interest and tax (PBIT) is the same as operating profit.

Interest cover is expressed as a number, e.g. 4 times. It gives an indication of how easily the organisation can maintain payments of its loan and debenture interest and therefore gives additional information about the riskiness of the organisation.

A rough guide would be to assume that if the interest cover is 2 times then we can assume that profit could halve and interest payments can still be made. Anything lower than 2 would indicate a risky situation.

Interest cover and gearing (see below) are two of the key ratios a bank will look at when deciding to provide new finance (e.g. a new loan or to extend an overdraft). These two ratios give a good indicator of the level of **risk** in a business.

High gearing and low interest cover would indicate high risk, which would concern a company's bank, and potentially its suppliers as well.

7 Debt ratios

7.1 Gearing ratio

Here we are trying to assess the composition of a company's capital structure – is the business being funded by equity (repayable to shareholders) or by debt (repayable to banks). If there is a lot of debt compared to the equity it is thought that a business is riskier as debt must be paid back to the banks when requested whereas equity does not have to be paid back to the shareholders on demand. The greater the extent to which a company is financed by debt, the greater is the risk involved in allowing it credit terms.

$$\text{Gearing ratio} = \frac{\text{Total debt}}{\text{Total debt + equity}} \times 100$$

Examination points:

- **Total debt should include all non current liabilities (loans) only. Short-term debt such as overdrafts are NOT to be included for the purposes of CRDM.**

8 Example and activities

8.1 Example

> **Example**
>
> The following illustration demonstrates some of the ratios with which you need to be familiar when assessing credit risk.
>
> **Summarised statement of financial position at 31 December 20X1**
>
> | | £000 | £000 |
> |---|---|---|
> | **Non-current assets**, at cost, less depreciation | | 2,600 |
> | **Current assets** | | |
> | Inventory | 600 | |
> | Trade receivables | 900 | |
> | Cash and other equivalents | 100 | |
> | | 1,600 | |
> | | | 1,600 |
> | **Total assets** | | **4,200** |
> | | | |
> | **Equity** | | |
> | Ordinary share capital (£1 shares) | | 1,000 |
> | Preference share capital | | 200 |
> | Retained earnings | | 800 |
> | | | 2,000 |
> | **Non-current liabilities** | | |
> | Loan | | 1,400 |
> | **Current liabilities** | | |
> | Trade payables | 800 | |
> | | | 800 |
> | **Total equity and liabilities** | | **4,200** |

Summarised statement of profit or loss for the year ended 31 December 20X1

	20X1
	£000
Revenue	6,000
Cost of sales	(4,000)
Gross profit	2,000
Operating expenses	(1,660)
Operating profit	340
Finance cost	(74)
Profit before tax	266
Taxation	(106)
	160
Preference dividend	(10)
Profit for the year	150

Note that cost of sales and operating expenses include £600,000 of depreciation charges.

Solution

Liquidity ratios

Current ratio

$$\text{Current ratio} = \frac{\text{Current assets}}{\text{Current liabilities}} = \frac{£1,600}{£800} = 2$$

Quick ratio

$$\text{Quick ratio} = \frac{\text{Current assets} - \text{Inventory}}{\text{Current liabilities}} = \frac{£1,600 - £600}{£800} = 1.25$$

Trade receivables collection period

$$\text{Trade receivables collection period} = \frac{\text{Trade receivables}}{\text{Sales revenue}} \times 365$$

$$= \frac{£900}{£6,000} \times 365 = 55 \text{ days}$$

Trade payable collection period

$$\text{Trade payable payment period} = \frac{\text{Trade payables}}{\text{Cost of sales}} \times 365$$

$$= \frac{£800}{£4,000 \text{ (CoS)}} \times 365 = 73 \text{ days}$$

Inventory holding period in days

$$\text{Inventory holding period} = \frac{\text{Inventory}}{\text{Cost of sales}} \times 365$$

$$= \frac{£600}{£4,000} \times 365 = 55 \text{ days}$$

Working capital cycle

Inventory holding period + receivables collection period – payables collection period = 55 + 55 – 73 = 37 days

Profitability ratios

Gross profit margin

$$\text{Margin} = \frac{\text{Gross profit}}{\text{Sales revenue}} \times 100 = \frac{£2,000}{£6,000} \times 100 = 33.33\%$$

Operating profit margin

$$\text{Margin} = \frac{\text{Operating profit}}{\text{Sales revenue}} \times 100$$

$$= \frac{£340}{£6,000} \times 100 = 5.67\%$$

Interest cover

$$\text{Finance charge cover} = \frac{\text{Profit before interest and tax}}{\text{Interest payable}}$$

$$= \frac{£340}{£74} = 4.6 \text{ times}$$

Return on capital employed

$$\text{Return on capital employed} = \frac{\text{Operating profit}}{\text{Capital employed}} \times 100$$

$$= \frac{£340}{£2,000 + £1,400} \times 100 = 10\%$$

Gearing ratio

$$\text{Gearing ratio} = \frac{\text{Total debt}}{\text{Total debt + equity}} \times 100$$

$$= \frac{£1,400}{£2,000 + £1,400} \times 100 = 41.18\%$$

8.2 Activities

> ### Test your understanding 7
>
> **Summarised statement of financial position at 31 December 20X1**
>
> | | £000 | £000 |
> |---|---|---|
> | **Non-current assets**, at cost, less depreciation | | 2,500 |
> | **Current assets** | | |
> | Inventory | 900 | |
> | Trade receivables | 800 | |
> | Cash and other equivalents | 300 | |
> | | | 2,000 |
> | **Total assets** | | **4,500** |
> | **Equity** | | |
> | Ordinary shares (£1 shares) | | 1,000 |
> | Preference shares | | 250 |
> | General reserve | | 600 |
> | Retained earnings | | 150 |
> | | | 2,000 |
> | **Non-current liabilities** | | |
> | 10% debentures (loan) | | 1,500 |
> | **Current liabilities** | | |
> | Trade payables | 700 | |
> | Other payables | 300 | |
> | | | 1,000 |
> | **Total equity and liabilities** | | **4,500** |

Statement of profit or loss for year ended 31 December 20X1

	£000	£000
Revenue		6,000
Cost of sales		
Inventory at 1 January 20X1	500	
Purchases	4,000	
	———	
	4,500	
Less: inventory at 31 December 20X1	(900)	
	———	
		(3,600)
		———
Gross profit		2,400
Administrative expenses and distribution costs		(1,830)
		———
Operating profit		570
Finance cost		(150)
		———
Profit before tax		420
Taxation		(210)
		———
		210
Preference dividend		(10)
		———
Profit for the year		200
		———

Required

Calculate:

- Return on capital employed
- Operating profit margin
- Current ratio
- Quick ratio
- Trade receivable days
- Trade payable days
- Inventory days
- Working capital cycle
- Gearing ratio
- Interest cover.

One set of performance indicator calculations is not really enough to draw conclusions from. Many companies will request a couple of years of accounts to perform calculations on to see how the business under investigation has changed. Another method is to have a credit rating (scoring) system to be able to grade a company's credit risk.

Test your understanding 8

The accounts of Falcon Limited for the years ended 30 June 20X3 and 30 June 20X2 are as follows.

Statement of financial position

	20X3		20X2	
	£	£	£	£
Non-current assets				
Property		140,000		80,000
Plant		130,000		70,000
		270,000		150,000
Current assets				
Inventory	120,000		100,000	
Trade receivables	80,000		60,000	
		200,000		160,000
Total assets		470,000		310,000
Equity				
£1 ordinary shares		100,000		50,000
Share premium account		90,000		35,000
Retained earnings		135,000		120,000
		325,000		205,000
Non-current liabilities				
7% Loan		65,000		55,000
Current liabilities				
Trade payables	45,000		30,000	
Overdraft	15,000		5,000	
Taxation	20,000		15,000	
		80,000		50,000
Total equity and liabilities		470,000		310,000

Statement of profit or loss

	20X3 £	20X2 £
Revenue	525,000	425,000
Operating profit	53,500	41,000
Finance cost	(3,500)	(3,500)
Profit before tax	50,000	37,500
Tax	(20,000)	(15,000)
	30,000	22,500
Dividends	(15,000)	(10,000)
Profit for the year	15,000	12,500

Credit rating (scoring) system	Score
Operating profit margin	
losses	−5
less than 5%	0
5% and above but less than 10%	5
10% and above but less than 20%	10
more than 20%	20
Interest cover	
no cover	−30
less than 1	−20
more than 1 but less than 2	−10
more than 2 but less than 4	0
more than 4	10
Current ratio	
less than 1	−20
between 1 and 1.25	−10
between 1.25 and 1.5	0
above 1.5	10

Gearing	
less than 25%	20
25% and above but less than 50%	10
more than 50% less than 65%	0
between 65% and 75%	−20
between 75% and 80%	−40
above 80%	−100
Risk	**aggregate score**
very low risk	Between 60 and 21
low risk	Between 20 and 1
medium risk	Between 0 and −24
high risk	Between −25 and −50
very high risk	Above −50

Required

Calculate the performance indicators listed below and using the credit rating system calculate the risk of having Falcon Limited as a credit customer.

	Indicator	Rating	Indicator	Rating
Year	20X3		20X2	
Operating profit margin				
Interest cover				
Current ratio				
Gearing				
Total				

Test your understanding 9

Jacket and Tie have been trading with your company for several years and has, until recently, always paid to terms. Recently there have been a couple of late payments and Jacket and Tie have contacted you asking to increase their credit limit from £50,000 to £75,000.

Jacket and Tie have supplied the accounts below:

Statement of profit or loss

	20X1 £	20X2 £
Sales revenue	350,000	230,000
Cost of sales	(227,500)	(149,500)
Gross profit	122,500	80,500
Distribution costs	(25,000)	(20,000)
Administration costs	(50,000)	(45,000)
Operating profit	47,500	15,500
Finance cost	(5,000)	(5,000)
Profit before tax	42,500	10,500
Tax	(6,000)	(5,000)
Profit for the year	36,500	5,500

Statement of financial position

	20X1 £	20X2 £
Non-current assets	71,959	100,000
Current assets		
Inventory	25,690	18,164
Trade receivables	62,789	41,918
Cash	35,878	500
	124,357	60,582
Total assets	196,316	160,582
Equity		
Share capital	70,000	70,000
Retained earnings	43,418	22,418
	113,418	92,418
Non-current liabilities		
Loans	36,959	50,000
Current liabilities		
Short term loan	21,959	
Trade payable	23,980	18,164
	45,939	18,164
Total equity and liabilities	196,316	160,582

Jacket and Tie have also provided you with some further information:

We have recently succeeded in securing the business of several new large clients so we have had to purchase new assets with a long term loan to ensure that we can meet demand.

We expect sales to increase next year but for our costs to stay constant as we are able to reduce variable costs through the use of our new machines.

Using the template provided:

1   Calculate the key indicators for the current and previous years for Jacket and Tie.

Jacket and Tie	Indicator 20X1	Indicator 20X2
Operating profit margin		
Interest cover		
Current ratio		
Gearing		
Trade receivable days		
Trade payable days		

2   Analyse the ratios and the financial statements and discuss whether extension of the credit limit is feasible. You may want to consider adding terms to the contract.

Test your understanding 10

You work as a credit controller and Sort Me Out Limited is asking for credit terms. They would like a credit limit of £750,000. Sort Me Out Limited have provided their financial accounts for the last two years.

Statement of profit or loss	20X2	20X1
	£000	£000
Revenue	5,500	6,500
Cost of sales	3,500	3,800
Gross profit	2,000	2,700
Distribution costs	1,250	2,150
Administration costs	1,000	1,000
Operating profit	−250	−450
Interest payable	50	50
Profit before taxation	−300	−500
Tax	0	0
Profit for the year	−300	−500

Statement of financial position	20X2	20X1
	£000	£000
Non-current assets		
Tangible assets	3,200	3,500
Current assets		
Inventories	1,000	800
Trade receivables	1,100	950
Cash	100	500
	2,200	2,250
Total assets	5,400	5,750
Equity		
Share capital	200	200
Retained earnings	1,900	3,050
	2,100	3,250
Non-current liabilities		
Long term loans	1,000	500
Current liabilities		
Trade payables	2,300	2,000
Total liabilities	3,300	2,500
Total equity and liabilities	5,400	5,750

Credit rating (scoring) system	Score
Operating profit margin	
losses	–5
less than 5%	0
5% and above but less than 10%	5
10% and above but less than 20%	10
20% and above	20
Interest cover	
no cover	–30
less than 1	–20
1 and above but less than 2	–10
2 and above but less than 4	0
4 and above	10
Current ratio	
less than 1	–20
1 and above and less than 1.25	–10
1.25 and above and less than 1.5	0
1.5 and above	10
Gearing	
less than 25%	20
25% and above but less than 50%	10
50% and above and less than 65%	0
65% and above and less than 75%	–20
75% and above and less than 80%	–40
80% and above	–100

Risk	aggregate score
very low risk	Between 60 and 21
low risk	Between 20 and 1
medium risk	Between 0 and –24
high risk	Between –25 and –50
very high risk	Above –50

Calculate the performance indicators below for Sort Me Out Limited

Sort Me Out Limited	Indicator	Rating	Indicator	Rating
Year	20X2		20X1	
Operating profit margin				
Interest cover				
Current ratio				
Gearing				
Total				

Will we offer credit terms to Sort Me Out Limited?

9 Overtrading

9.1 Overtrading

It is entirely possible for a profitable business to run short of cash. For example, a business may be making a profit but it has to replace a large item of machinery and this will deplete its cash resources to the extent that it may not be able to pay its payables when they fall due. In the worst case scenario this might even mean that the business is forced into liquidation.

It is also possible that a business may be **Overtrading. Overtrading** usually occurs when a business tries to **expand too quickly** and **over-stretches its working capital** due to inadequate financing for its growth rate. If **sales increase too rapidly**, then working capital requirements may increase as **more money is tied up in inventories** of raw materials to support the increased sales levels; **receivables will also rise**.

This can lead to a situation in which the business is operating at a profit but suffers a liquidity crisis as it has insufficient cash to pay its bills and expenses.

This problem happens over a period of time, with the working capital gradually being stretched and without the managers of the business realising what is happening as the company continues to be profitable. The statement of financial position eventually reveals the problem.

9.2 Identifying signs of overtrading

Through analysis of a set of accounts it may be possible to identify signs of overtrading as follows:

- sharply and rapidly increasing sales volumes
- large decline in cash levels
- falling profit margins despite increased sales as higher discounts are given to attract more customers and production costs increase due to overtime costs, etc
- greater reliance on short-term funding such as overdrafts
- longer receivable/payable collection ratios.

9.3 Controlling overtrading

Planned overtrading is not dangerous; it is the unmanaged and undetected overtrading that causes company downfalls.

If, however, the symptoms of unmanaged overtrading are detected, then the problem may be averted by:

- issuing new share capital or loan stock
- taking out long-term loans rather than overdrafts
- reducing the operating cycle by controlling receivables and payables
- slowing down the company's expansion.

9.4 Over-capitalisation

If there are excessive inventories, trade receivable and cash, and very few trade payables, there will be an over-investment by the company in current assets. This is the opposite of overtrading – working capital will be excessive and the company will be over-capitalised.

Test your understanding 11

You work as a credit controller and Help Me Out Limited is asking for credit terms. They would like a credit limit of £750,000. Help Me Out Limited has provided their financial accounts for the two previous years.

Statement of financial position

	20X1	20X0
	£000	£000
Non-current assets		
Property, plant and equipment	7,000	4,000
Current assets		
Inventory	1,000	500
Receivables	1,100	700
Cash	200	500
	2,300	1,700
Total assets	9,300	5,700
Equity		
Share capital	150	150
Retained earnings	2,500	2,600
	2,650	2,750
Non-current liabilities		
Borrowing	5,500	2,500
Current liabilities		
Trade payables	1,150	450
Total liabilities	6,650	2,950
Total equity and liabilities	9,300	5,700

Statement of profit or loss

	20X1	20X0
	£000	£000
Revenue	6,000	5,000
Cost of sales	4,500	3,000
Gross profit	1,500	2,000
Distribution and administration expenses	1,200	1,200
Operating profit	300	800
Finance cost	550	200
Profit before taxation	−250	600
Taxation	0	150
Profit for the year	−250	450

Complete the table below by calculating the key indicators (to 2 decimal places)

	20X1	20X0
Operating profit margin		
Interest cover		
Trade receivable collection period in days		
Trade payable payment period in days		
Inventory holding period in days		
Current ratio		
Gearing		

Write a brief note to explain whether Help Me Out plc is overtrading by stating the signs of overtrading and considering Help Me Out's performance indicators.

10 Credit terms and conditions

10.1 Introduction

Once a potential trade receivable has been analysed and it has been agreed that they can be offered credit then communication with them is required regarding a number of issues.

It will be necessary to request information from the new trade receivable to be able to **set up a credit account**. This includes:

- confirmation of name
- confirmation of address
- amount they want to be able to buy on credit
- VAT registration number (if applicable).

It is also necessary to agree the **terms and conditions** of the credit agreement (contract). Credit terms have to be drawn up for a business and must take into account the need to maintain both the businesses' cash flow and a sensible profit margin on the goods sold.

These terms must be **clearly understood** by the customer and it is sensible to print these clearly on the invoice to the customer. The business must be prepared to enforce the terms if the customer is late paying the debt.

KAPLAN PUBLISHING

Definitions

- **Credit limit** – the maximum value that may be outstanding.

- **Credit term** – the length of time amounts can be outstanding for.

When determining a credit limit it is necessary to consider the number and value of the orders the sales team expects during the credit term.

 Example

The sales team expects weekly orders of £1,000.

The credit term is 30 days.

What would be a sensible credit limit?

If we assume that 4 weeks make up the 30 days than we would be prudent to set a credit limit between £4,000 and £5,000.

10.2 A typical credit control policy and procedure

Credit terms and conditions should be laid out in a document which should be available to new and current trade receivables to review.

A typical credit control policy could be as follows:

New accounts

- One bank reference and two trade references are required.

- A credit reference agency report and the last three years published accounts for limited companies need to be analysed.

- A credit reference agency report and the last three years accounts for a sole trader need to be analysed.

Existing customers

- A credit reference agency report to be obtained on an annual basis together with the latest annual accounts (either from Companies' House or directly from the customer). Both documents to be reviewed.

- A trading history review to be undertaken annually to review for performance against credit limits and terms of payments.

- Annual review of usage of the customer's credit limit to ensure that an outdated credit limit is not in existence. This is particularly important where the trade with the customer has reduced over the past year.

Credit terms

- Standard terms are 30 days from invoice. Any extension to be authorised by the Finance Director.

- A 2% settlement discount to be offered to all accounts with a profit margin of 50% or greater, or with a profit margin of 30% and a value in excess of £50,000 or with the credit controllers discretion.

Debt collection process

- Invoices to be despatched on day of issue, (day of issue to be no more than 2 days after date of delivery).

- Statements to be despatched in the second week of the month.

- Aged trade receivable analysis to be produced and reviewed on a weekly basis.

- Reminder letter to be sent once an account is overdue.

- Telephone chaser for accounts 15 days overdue.

- Customer on stop list if no payment is received within 5 days of the telephone chaser. Computerised sales order processing system updated and automatic email sent to the customer contact and the account manager (sales person).

- Letter threatening legal action if payment not received within 30 days of the first letter.

- Legal proceedings/debt collection agency instructed subject to the approval of the Finance Director.

- Prepare a report suggesting an appropriate provision for irrecoverable or doubtful debts.

If at any stage in the process the customer is declared insolvent or bankrupt then contact the insolvency practitioner in order to register the debt and notify the financial accountant so that the VAT can be reclaimed.

Other things that would be discussed include:

- if there will be a **settlement discount** for prompt or early payment

- it will be necessary to agree how **payment** will be made

- **credit insurance**

- any **legal conditions** within the contract such as 'Retention of Title'.

10.3 Communication with trade receivables

There are a number of ways that a company can communicate with a trade receivable. Each method may be used as part of the set up checks or as an on-going method of managing trade receivables.

Face to Face communications are required:

- if there is a big contract being formed there is likely to be a face to face meeting to discuss and agree prices and payment schedule

- if there is a query over an invoice

- to confirm the existence of the company in question.

Telecommunications would include:

- telephone – telephone calls are a **quick way** of making personal contact and of obtaining an immediate response

- email – quick method of communication, can get delivery and read receipts on emails, good for audit trail of conversations

- internet – use to display credit control policy, any price changes.

Written communication would include:

- invoices – sent when goods/services delivered

- statements – sent once a month to show status of account

- letters – sent when needed i.e. to chase up payment, from solicitors etc.

Visits to trade receivables can be useful for:

- assessing their ability to pay

- in sorting out any administrative problems

- **establishing good relations** with key personnel.

Throughout all the communications with customers, it is important to remember that the **aim is to persuade them to pay their bill**. A firm approach is needed in all dealings to ensure this message is understood. Credit controllers should act with authority as late payment is in breach of the credit terms.

It is important that people with good interpersonal skills communicate with the customer to avoid unnecessary acrimony.

It is also important that pursuit of the customer is discreet and confidential. Broadcasting to the business community that a certain business is not paying its bills can have severe effects on that business, and may even result in libel writs.

11 Refusal of credit

11.1 Introduction

In some instances, after assessing a company, the credit manager may decide that it is not possible to trade with a new customer on credit terms.

11.2 Possible reasons for refusal of credit

The decision to refuse to grant credit to a new customer is a big decision for the credit manager as the business will not wish to lose this potential customer's business, but the credit manager will have taken a view that the risk of non-payment from the customer is too high for credit terms to be granted.

Refusal of credit does not necessarily mean that the potential customer's business is bad or is likely not to survive; it simply means that based on the evidence available to the credit manager the risk of non-payment is too high.

There are a variety of reasons why a credit manager may decide against granting of credit which include the following:

- a non-committal or poor bank reference

- poor trade references

- concerns about the validity of any trade references submitted

- adverse press comment about the potential customer

- poor credit agency report

- indications of business weakness from analysis of the financial statements

- lack of historical financial statements due to being a recently started company.

The credit manager will consider all of the evidence available about a potential customer and the reason for the refusal of credit may be due to a single factor noted above or a combination of factors.

11.3 Communication of refusal of credit

If credit is not to be granted to a potential customer then this must be communicated (usually in writing) in a **tactful and diplomatic manner**.

The key points to remember when communicating refusal of credit are:

- be polite and explain **why** credit is being refused

- explain that you would be happy to reassess the situation in the future, and **what the company needs to do in order to obtain credit**

- you are happy to trade with the customer on **cash terms** in the meantime.

 Example

You are the credit manager for Howard Ltd and your name is Belinda Sean. You have recently been assessing requests for credit from two potential new customers.

Fisher Ltd – this company has requested credit limit of £5,000 from your company and 30 days' credit. Two trade references have been provided (but no bank reference), along with the last set of published financial statements which include the previous years' comparative figures. The trade references appeared satisfactory although one is from Barnaby & Sons and it has been noted that the managing director of Fisher Ltd is Mr R Barnaby.

Analysis of the financial statements has indicated a decrease in profitability during the last year, a high level of gearing and low liquidity ratios.

Jacob Enterprises Ltd – this company is requesting 30 days of credit and a credit limit of £4,000. They have provided their statement of financial position at their year-end which was four months ago and the statement of profit or loss for the year to that date. The financial statements indicate fairly low levels of profitability but there is nothing to compare the figures to. The bank reference is satisfactory but of the two trade references one has only been trading with Jacob Enterprises for two months.

You are to draft suitable letters to each potential customer.

HOWARD LTD
Dene Court
Dene Park
Hereford
HF3 9RT

Finance Director
Fisher Ltd
Farm Road Industrial Park
Fordtown

Dear Sir

Re: Request for credit facilities

Thank you for your enquiry regarding the provision of credit facilities by us for £5,000 of credit on 30 day terms. We have taken up your trade references and examined your latest set of financial statements.

We are unfortunately concerned about your levels of profitability in the most recent year and also have some concerns about one of the trade references from Barnaby & Sons.

On balance we are not in a position to grant your request for trade credit at the current time, although we would of course be delighted to trade with you on a cash basis. If you do not wish to trade on this basis and would like to enquire about credit terms in the future then we would be delighted to examine your current year's financial statements when they are available.

Thank you for your interest in our company.

Yours faithfully

Belinda Sean

Belinda Sean
Credit Manager

HOWARD LTD
Dene Court
Dene Park
Hereford
HF3 9RT

Finance Director
Jacob Enterprises Ltd
White Hill
Blacktown

Dear Madam

Re: Request for credit facilities

Thank you for your enquiry regarding the provision of credit facilities by us for £4,000 of credit on 30 day terms. We have taken up your trade references and examined your latest set of financial statements.

We have some concerns about your level of profitability and would like the opportunity to examine your statement of financial position and statement of profit or loss for the two previous years. As one of your trade references has only been trading with you for two months, we would request details of a further supplier that we could contact for a trade reference.

At this stage I am unable to confirm whether we can provide you with a credit facility but will reconsider the situation when we receive your financial statements and additional trade reference.

Thank you for your interest in our company and in the meantime we would of course be delighted to trade with you on a cash terms basis.

Yours faithfully

Belinda Sean

Belinda Sean
Credit Manager

Test your understanding 12

You are the credit manager for Style Ltd and your name is Yusuf Hoover. You have recently been assessing requests for credit from potential new customers.

NY Partners have requested to purchase goods from you, would like a £4,000 credit limit and 60 days' credit. You asked for trade references and bank references and financial statements for the last three years. They have provided you with a bank reference which states that 'the partnership appears to be well constituted but we cannot necessarily speak for your figures due to the length of time that the partnership has been in operation'. They have also provided one trade reference which is satisfactory from a company which allows NY Partners £2,000 of credit on 30-day terms. However, the partnership has only been in operation for nine months and therefore they have not been able to provide you with any financial statements.

You are to draft a suitable letter to this potential customer.

Test your understanding 13

A new customer, Crust Limited, has asked your company for credit terms. Your company has a policy of carrying out an analysis of a customer's financial statements as a part of an internal credit checking exercise, before deciding whether to agree to granting credit. Crust Limited has requested a credit limit of £30,000.

You have been given the financial statements of Crust Limited (extracts shown below).

Extracts of accounts of Crust Limited

	Current year	Previous year
Statement of profit and loss	£	£
Revenue	3,100,000	3,350,000
Cash operating expenses	2,400,000	2,700,000
Operating profit	105,000	53,000
Finance cost	4,000	3,000
Statement of financial position		
Non-current assets	315,000	395,000
Current assets		
Inventory	62,000	66,000
Receivables	75,000	86,000
Cash and short-term investments	30,000	8,000
	167,000	160,000
Total assets	**482,000**	**555,000**
Equity		
Share capital	100,000	100,000
Retained earnings	225,000	260,000
Retained for the year	35,000	22,000
	360,000	382,000

Non-current liabilities		
Bank loans	45,000	58,000
Current liabilities		
Bank overdraft	5,000	28,000
Trade payables	70,000	75,000
Other payables	2,000	12,000
	77,000	115,000
Total equity and liability	**482,000**	**555,000**

Credit rating (scoring) system	Score
Operating profit margin	
losses	–5
less than 5%	0
5% and above but less than 10%	5
10% and above but less than 20%	10
more than 20%	20
Interest cover	
no cover	–30
less than 1	–20
more than 1 but less than 2	–10
more than 2 but less than 4	0
more than 4	10
Current ratio	
less than 1	–20
between 1 and 1.25	–10
between 1.25 and 1.5	0
above 1.5	10
Gearing	
less than 25%	20
25% and above but less than 50%	10
more than 50% less than 65%	0
between 65% and 75%	–20
between 75% and 80%	–40
above 80%	–100

Risk	Aggregate score
very low risk	Between 60 and 21
low risk	Between 20 and 1
medium risk	Between 0 and –24
high risk	Between –25 and –50
very high risk	Above –50

Using the template provided:

1   Calculate the key indicators for the current and previous years for Crust Limited.

2   Rate the company using the credit rating (scoring system) provided above.

Crust Limited	Indicator current year	Rating	Indicator previous year	Rating
Operating profit margin				
Interest cover				
Current ratio				
Gearing				
Total rating				

3   Based on your results recommend, with reasons, whether the requested credit limit should be given to Crust Limited.

4   If credit is being refused draft a letter to Crust Limited communicating the decision and explain what action the company could take to improve its chance of being granted credit in the future. If credit is being allowed prepare a telephone script which could be used by the person contacting the company to communicate the decision.

Test your understanding 14

You work as a credit control manager for Trafford Limited which uses a credit rating system to assess the credit status of new and existing customers.

The credit rating (scoring) system table below is used to assess the risk of default by calculating key indicators (ratios), comparing them to the table and calculating an aggregate score.

Credit rating (scoring) system	Score
Gross profit margin	
losses	–6
less than 20%	–3
20% and above but less than 40%	0
40% or above	3
Current ratio	
Less than 0.75	–6
More than or equal to 0.75 but less than 1.25	–3
More than or equal to 1.25 but less than 1.75	0
1.75 or above	3
Credit rating (scoring) system	Score
Payable days	
90 days or above	–3
More than 60 but less than 90 days	0
More than 30 days but less than 60 days	3
Less than 30 days	6
Gearing	
less than or equal to 30%	3
more than 30% but less than or equal to 40%	0
more than 40% but less than or equal to 50%	–6
more than 50%	–12

Risk	aggregate score
very low risk	Higher than 6
low risk	Between 6 and 1
medium risk	Between 0 and –7
high risk	Between –8 and –15
very high risk	Worse than –15

Existing customer requesting an increase in their credit limit

The sales department has asked for the credit limit of Alty Limited, an existing customer, to be extended from £50,000 to £100,000. The financial information below has been supplied by Alty Limited.

Statement of profit or loss	20X1	20X0
	£000	£000
Revenue	4,500	5,000
Cost of sales	2,750	2,000
Gross profit	1,750	3,000
Distribution costs	500	600
Administration costs	600	500
Operating profit	650	1,900
Finance cost	350	100
Profit before taxation	300	1,800
Tax	100	200
Profit for the year	200	1,600

Statement of financial position	20X1	20X0
	£000	£000
Non-current assets		
Property, plant and equipment	4,900	2,600
Current assets		
Inventory	400	300
Trade receivables	600	900
Cash	0	50
	1,000	1,250
Total assets	5,900	3,850
Equity		
Share capital	500	500
Retained earnings	1,700	1,500
	2,200	2,000
Non-current liabilities		
Loans	1,650	1,250
Current liabilities		
Trade payables	400	600
Overdraft	1,650	0
	2,050	600
Total equity and liabilities	5,900	3,850

New customer request form

The sales department has asked for a credit limit of £150,000 to be given to Hale Limited who is a potential new customer. The financial information below has been supplied by Hale Limited.

Statement of profit or loss	20X1	20X0
	£000	£000
Revenue	10,000	9,500
Cost of sales	4,000	4,275
Gross profit	6,000	5,225
Distribution costs	1,100	1,000
Administration costs	2,000	1,500
Operating profit	2,900	2,725
Finance cost	700	600
Profit before taxation	2,200	2,125
Tax	200	200
Profit for the year	2,000	1,925

Statement of financial position	20X1	20X0
	£000	£000
Non-current assets		
Property, plant and equipment	7,250	4,400
Current assets		
Inventory	400	400
Trade receivables	750	700
Cash	100	400
	1,250	1,500
Total assets	8,500	5,900
Equity		
Share capital	1,000	1,000
Retained earnings	4,000	2,000
	5,000	3,000
Non-current liabilities		
Loans	2,500	2,000
Current liabilities		
Trade payables	1,000	900
Total equity and liabilities	8,500	5,900

Required:

Using the templates provided to two decimal places:

(i) Calculate the key indicators for 20X0 and 20X1 for Alty Limited and Hale Limited, and

(ii) Rate each company using the credit rating (scoring) system.

Based on the results of your credit rating, recommend, with reasons, whether the requested credit limits should be given to Alty Limited and Hale Limited.

Where the request for credit is being refused, draft a note or a letter communicating the decision and explaining what action the company could take to improve its chances of being accepted in the future.

Alty Limited	Indicator	Rating	Indicator	Rating
Year	20X1		20X0	
Gross profit margin %				
Current ratio				
Trade payables days				
Gearing %				
Total				

Hale Limited	Indicator	Rating	Indicator	Rating
Year	20X1		20X0	
Gross profit margin %				
Current ratio				
Trade payables days				
Gearing %				
Total				

11.4 Trial period for credit

In some cases there may be some concerns about the information available about a potential new customer, but perhaps not enough of a concern to refuse to grant credit. In such circumstances it might be appropriate to **grant a degree of credit to the customer on a trial basis** with review of the situation at some point in the future.

For example, if a potential customer's trade references show that in one case although the customer has been given 30 days of credit they generally take 60 days to pay, then your company may offer them a fairly low credit limit on 30-day terms and monitor the situation for, say, six months when the situation will be re-assessed.

 Example

You are again the credit manager for Howard Ltd and your name is Belinda Sean. You have been assessing the financial statements for Reed & Sons who have requested £6,000 of credit on 60-day terms. You also have received a satisfactory bank reference and trade references.

Your analysis of the 20X3 and 20X2 financial statements show the following picture:

	20X3	20X2
Gross profit margin	28%	30%
Net profit margin	4%	3%
Interest cover	1.5 times	0.9 times
Current ratio	1.3 times	0.8 times

You are to draft a suitable letter to Reed & Sons dealing with their request for credit facilities.

Solution

HOWARD LTD
Dene Court
Dene Park
Hereford
HF3 9RT

Finance Director
Reed & Sons
Ghyll Farm Development
Steel Cross

Dear Sir

Re: Request for credit facilities

Thank you for your enquiry regarding the provision of credit facilities by us for £6,000 of credit on 60 day terms. We have taken up your bank and trade references and examined your latest set of financial statements.

Although your references are satisfactory, we have some concerns about your profitability and liquidity. Clearly, your overall profitability and liquidity position have improved since 20X2 but their levels are still lower than we would normally accept in order to grant a credit facility.

However, due to your bank and trade references, we would be happy to offer you a credit facility for six months at the end of which period the movement on your account would be reviewed and the position re-assessed. The credit limit that we could offer you would initially be £2,000 and the payment terms would be strictly 30 days from the invoice date.

Thank you for your interest in our company and we look forward to trading with you on the basis set out above.

Yours sincerely

Belinda Sean

Belinda Sean
Credit Manager

12 Summary

In this chapter we have considered the question of whether to grant credit to a customer and how much credit to grant.

The decision as to whether to grant credit should be based upon external information such as references and also internal information created from ratio analysis of a customer's financial statements. After all of this information has been considered, a final decision can be made as to whether or not to grant the customer credit terms.

Test your understanding answers

 Test your understanding 1

Answer A – Offering credit is likely to increase expenses (credit control department, additional admin costs, greater reliance on an overdraft).

 Test your understanding 2

Answer B

 Test your understanding 3

Answer B – All the others come from sources outside of your business.

 Test your understanding 4

Answer A – Aged **payables** is about your suppliers, not your customers.

 Test your understanding 5

Answer C – Wil a new customer there will not be any aged receivable information or outstanding invoices.

 Test your understanding 6

Answer B

Test your understanding 7

Return on capital employed	$(570/3{,}500) \times 100$	$= 16.3\%$
Operating profit margin	$(570/6{,}000) \times 100$	$= 9.5\%$
Current ratio	$2{,}000/1{,}000$	$= 2$
Quick ratio	$1{,}100/1{,}000$	$= 1.1$
Receivable days	$(800/6{,}000) \times 365$	$= 49$ days
Payable days	$(700/3{,}600) \times 365$	$= 71$ days
Inventory days	$(900/3{,}600) \times 365$	$= 91$ days
Working capital cycle	$91 + 49 - 71$	$= 69$ days
Gearing ratio (total debt/total debt + equity	$(1{,}500/3{,}500) \times 100$	$= 42.9\%$
Interest cover	$570/150$	$= 3.8$ times

Test your understanding 8

Operating profit margin

20X3	20X2
$(53{,}500/525{,}000) \times 100 = 10.19\%$	$(41{,}000/425{,}000) \times 100 = 9.65\%$

Interest cover

20X3	20X2
$53{,}500/3{,}500 = 15.3$ times	$41{,}000/3{,}500 = 11.7$ times

Current ratio

20X3	20X2
$200{,}000/80{,}000 = 2.5$	$160{,}000/50{,}000 = 3.2$

Gearing ratio

20X3	20X2
$65{,}000/(325{,}000 + 65{,}000) \times 100 = 16.67\%$	$55{,}000/(205{,}000 + 55{,}000) \times 100 = 21.15\%$

	Indicator	Rating	Indicator	Rating
Year	20X3		20X2	
Operating profit margin	10.19%	10	9.65%	5
Interest cover	15.3	10	11.7	10
Current ratio	2.5	10	3.2	10
Gearing	16.67%	20	21.15%	20
Total		50		45

Falcon Limited is very low risk and should be allowed credit terms.

Test your understanding 9

Jacket and Tie	Indicator 20X1	Indicator 20X2
Operating profit margin	13.6%	6.7%
Interest cover	9.5	3.1
Current ratio	2.7	3.3
Gearing (D/D+E)	24.6%	35.1%
Trade receivable days	65.5	66.5
Trade payable days	38.5	44.3

Workings for Indicators

Indicator	20X1	20X2
Operating profit margin	47,500/350,000 × 100	15,500/230,000 × 100
Interest cover	47,500/5,000	15,500/5,000
Current ratio	124,357/45,939	60,582/18,164
Gearing (D/D+E)	36,959/ (36,959 + 113,418) × 100	50,000/(50,000 + 92,418) × 100
Receivable days	62,789/350,000 × 365	41,918/230,000 × 365
Payable days	23,980/227,500 × 365	18,164/149,500 × 365

Note: The following answer is exhaustive you would not be required to cover all the points mentioned to gain all the marks available.

Jacket and Tie have been trading with us for a number of years and has always met terms until recently. The overall picture from the financial statements is that Jacket and Tie may be having a few problems financially as revenue and overall profit have declined significantly.

The operating profit margin and interest cover have both declined from 20X1 to 20X2. This is due to the decrease in sales revenue, which has dropped by 34% from X1 to X2. The cost of sales, the distribution and administrative costs have all remained approximately at the same proportion when compared to sales revenue. For example the cost of sales as a percentage of revenue in both X1 and X2 is 65%, the distribution costs as a percentage of revenue in X1 is 7% and X2 is 9%, the administration costs as a percentage of revenue in X1 is 14% and in X2 is 20%.

The current ratio has improved but when the SOFP is considered it can be seen that the cash position has declined significantly. This may be due to the company repaying the short term loan during 20X2 but it does not account for all of decrease in the cash.

The majority of the current assets in 20X2 are trade receivables, which are the least liquid of the current assets; this could be explained by the introduction of the new large clients as these are likely to be credit customers. There does not appear to be a problem with credit control. The receivables collection period has remained fairly static at around 66 days.

The trade payables payment period has increased and this ties in with their late payment of debts with us. The increase is not significant and once the new customers have started paying this may return to the 20X1 level as cash becomes more available.

The gearing ratio has increased but this can be explained by the introduction of a new long term loan to cover the purchase of the new non-current assets.

The company remains liquid and is maintaining adequate trade receivable and trade payable day ratios. If, as stated, revenue increases and variable costs are maintained then some improvement in these ratios should be seen.

If extension is to be granted I would recommend asking for some form of security, for example include a retention of title clause in the contract.

Test your understanding 10

Sort Me Out Limited	Indicator	Rating	Indicator	Rating
Year	20X2		20X1	
Operating profit margin	–4.55%	–5	–6.92%	–5
Interest cover	0	–30	0	–30
Current ratio	0.96	–20	1.13	–10
Gearing	32.26%	10	13.33%	20
Total		–45		–25

Will we offer credit terms to Sort Me Out Limited?

No. Sort me Out Limited's credit scoring is high risk in 20X1 and 20X2. We could still trade with them but only on a cash basis.

 Test your understanding 11

Help Me Out plc	20X1	20X0
Operating profit margin	300/6,000 × 100 = 5.00%	800/5,000 × 100 = 16.00%
Interest cover	300/550 = 0.55 times	800/200 = 4.00 times
Trade receivable collection period in days	1,100/6,000 × 365 = 66.92 days	700/5,000 × 365 = 51.10 days
Trade payable payment period in days	1,150/4,500 × 365 = 93.28 days	450/3,000 × 365 = 54.75 days
Inventory holding period in days	1,000/4,500 × 365 = 81.11 days	500/3,000 × 365 = 60.83 days
Current ratio	2,300/1,150 = 2.00	1,700/450 = 3.78
Gearing (debt/debt + equity)	5,500/8,150 × 100 = 67.48%	2,500/5,250 × 100 = 47.62%

The signs of overtrading are as follows:

* Rapidly increasing sales revenue normally linked to extended credit terms
* Reduced gross and operating margins
* Increased inventory and trade receivables days
* Reduction in cash or an increase in overdraft
* Increased trade payable days

Help Me Out's performance indicators:

- Revenue has increased by 20%

- Operating profit margin has decreased

- Gross profit margin has also declined (20X1 = 25% and 20X0 = 40%)

- Inventory levels have increased by 100% from X0 to X1 and the holding period has increased by 20 days

- Trade receivables have increased by over 50% from X0 to X1 and the collection period has increased by about 16 days

- Cash has reduced but is still positive

- Trade payables have increased by over 150% and the payment period has almost doubled

It is possible that Help Me Out plc is overtrading.

 Test your understanding 12

Dear Sir

Re: Request for credit facilities

Thank you for your enquiry regarding the provision of credit facilities by us for £4,000 of credit on 60 day terms. We have taken up your trade and bank references which you kindly sent details of.

We have some concerns about offering credit at this early stage of your business as there are, as yet, no financial statements for your business that we can examine. Therefore, at this stage we cannot provide you with credit facilities.

We would of course be delighted to trade with you on cash terms until we have had an opportunity to examine your first year's trading figures. Therefore, please send us a copy of your first year financial statements when they are available and in the meantime contact us if you would like to start trading on a cash basis.

Thank you for your interest in our company.

Yours faithfully

Test your understanding 13

Crust Limited	Indicator current year	Rating	Indicator previous year	Rating
Operating profit margin	3.4%	0	1.6%	0
Interest cover	26.3	10	17.7	10
Current ratio	2.2	10	1.4	0
Gearing	11.11%	20	13.18%	20
Total rating		40		30

Workings for Indicators

Indicator	Current year	Previous year
Operating profit margin	105,000/3,100,000 × 100	53,000/3,350,000 × 100
Interest cover	105,000/4,000	53,000/3,000
Current ratio	167,000/77,000	160,000/115,000
Gearing	45,000/(360,000 + 45,000) × 100	58,000/(382,000 + 58,000) × 100

Crust Limited is a very low risk for both sets of accounts analysed.

Draft notes for telephone call:

Ensure that conversation is with the relevant person.

Confirm that credit will be granted.

Request the information to be able to set up a credit account. This includes:

- confirmation of name and address

- VAT registration number.

It is also necessary to agree the terms and conditions of the credit agreement i.e. confirm credit terms and credit limit.

Other things that would be discussed include:

- if there will be a settlement discount for prompt or early payment

- how payment will be received

- any legal conditions within the contract such as 'Retention of Title'.

Test your understanding 14

Alty Limited	Indicator	Rating	Indicator	Rating
Year	20X1		20X0	
Gross profit margin %	38.89	0	60.00	3
Current ratio	0.49	–6	2.08	3
Trade payables days	53.09	3	109.50	–3
Gearing %	42.86	–6	38.46	0
		–9		3

Workings – Alty	Indicator	Indicator
Year	20X1	20X0
Gross profit margin %	1,750/4,500 × 100	3,000/5,000 × 100
Current ratio	1,000/2,050	1,250/600
Trade payables days	400/2,750 × 365	600/2,000 × 365
Gearing %	1,650/(1,650 + 2,200) × 100	1,250/(1,250 + 2,000) × 100

Hale Limited	Indicator	Rating	Indicator	Rating
Year	20X1		20X0	
Gross profit margin %	60.00	3	55.00	3
Current ratio	1.25	0	1.67	0
Trade payables days	91.25	–3	76.84	0
Gearing %	33.33	0	40.00	0
		0		3

Workings – Hale	Indicator	Indicator
Year	20X1	20X0
Gross profit margin %	6,000/10,000 × 100	5,225/9,500 × 100
Current ratio	1,250/1,000	1,500/900
Trade payables days	1,000/4,000 × 365	900/4,275 × 365
Gearing %	2,500/(2,500 + 5,000) × 100	2,000/(2,000 + 3,000) × 100

Alty Limited

- Alty was rated as low risk (borderline very low risk) in 20X0 explaining why credit was given.

- Alty has been impacted by the credit crunch, with declining revenue and rising costs in the Statement of profit or loss.

- The credit crunch has also impacted on Alty's ability to re-finance the long term loan, resulting in the company being financed more via an overdraft which is repayable on demand and considerably more expensive (evidenced by the increased finance cost in the Statement of profit or loss).

Alty is now rated as high risk suggesting that credit should be refused. In addition it is recommended that the current credit limit is reviewed with the following possible options:

- Remove the credit facility.

- Reduce the current credit limit to a much lower level.

- Possibly insist on retention of title clauses.

Recommendation:

- The credit limit should be reduced over the next few months until Alty can convince us that it has put in place steps to control its cost base and refinance the long term loan.

- If Alty fails to do this over the next few months, the credit facility should be removed.

Hale Limited

- Hale is rated as medium risk indicating that the credit request should also be refused, however, this decision is a marginal one. The score of 0 being on the border between low and medium risk.

- In addition in the prior year Hale's score was in the low risk area and during the year trading results and profit have improved, as has the gearing of the company.

- The main reason for the decline in score is the increase in trade payables days.

Therefore the following possible options exist:

- Refuse credit.

- Offer a lower credit limit than the £150,000 proposed.

Recommendation:

- An initial lower credit limit should be granted (£50,000, for example). Hale Limited should be encouraged to reduce their payables days before any increase is proposed.

- If trade payables days improve then further credit up to the £150,000 can be offered.

Refusal of credit – Alty Limited

Introduction:

- Increase refused due to concerns regarding refinancing of long term loan and the impact of the credit crunch on business.

- Credit limit will be reduced over the next few months until refinancing has occurred.

Action points for Alty to improve liquidity:

- Re-finance overdraft (as a long term loan) to reduce finance cost, and current ratio.

- Look at cost base to try to improve margins.

- Consider raising some equity finance to reduce gearing.

Other recommendations:

- Possibly insist on retention of title clauses.

Refusal to raise limit – Hale Limited

Introduction:

- £150,000 credit limit refused, however an initial smaller credit limit will be offered for example £50,000.

- Credit limit will be increased as Hale demonstrates prompt payment of amounts owing.

Action points for Hale to improve creditworthiness:

- Improve payment speed to trade payables.

Collection of debts

3

Introduction

In this chapter, we look at the cost of offering credit and the various methods of debt collection available.

ASSESSMENT CRITERIA
Methods for the management of debt (3.1)
Manage accounts receivables (3.2)
Techniques to manage liquidity (3.3)
Communicate with stakeholders using a professional and ethical approach (3.4)

CONTENTS

1   Cost of offering credit

2   Debt collection procedures

3   Credit control and the impact on cash flow and liquidity

4   Settlement discounts

5   Factoring

6   Invoice discounting

7   Credit insurance

1 Cost of offering credit

1.1 Introduction

There are a number of costs associated with offering credit terms to a customer:

- Finance cost.

- Non-payment of debts.

- Administrative costs.

The credit control team need to ensure that debts are collected promptly to ensure these costs are kept to a minimum.

1.2 Finance cost

The main cost to the company of granting trade credit is the **finance cost**. Trade receivables on the statement of financial position do not earn a return i.e. the cash is not in the company's bank account therefore it is not earning interest. This may lead to the company needing to raise extra finance to be able to pay bills e.g. use of an overdraft.

A company that demands cash on delivery will have the cash available to pay bills so should not need to use an overdraft in the same manner. A company giving trade credit is effectively financing its trade receivable balances all year round in a similar manner to inventory balances.

Example

Z buys an item for £20 on 1 January 20X6 and pays the company one year later on 31 December 20X6. The company earns a profit of £4 on each unit sold. The company has an overdraft, paying interest at 10%.

What profit does the company make from the sale of the unit after allowing for the cost of credit?

Solution

	£
Net profit on sale of one unit	4
Less: Interest on overdraft	
(£20 outstanding receipt × 10%)	(2)
Real profit after credit period costs	2

So the granting of one year's credit has reduced the company's profit margin by 50% which is a substantial cost to the company. A year's credit is longer than companies would grant but even a two month credit period costs a company a substantial percentage of the profit margin, i.e.:

	£
Net profit on sales	4.00
Less: Interest on overdraft	
(using simple interest) £20 × 10% × (2/12)	(0.33)
Real profit after credit period costs	3.67

i.e. (33p/400p) × 100% = 8.25% of the profit is lost.

In other words, it costs the company 8.25% to offer two months' credit to its customers.

If interest rates increase, then the cost of credit will also increase. The main board of directors needs to consider these facts when agreeing credit terms with the credit manager.

1.3 Non-payment of debts

A company granting trade credit may suffer **irrecoverable debts** as a customer may go out of business (go into liquidation) before paying what is due. This cannot happen to a business that does not offer credit to its customers as cash is required on delivery of the goods.

 Definition

An **irrecoverable debt** is a debt which the credit manager is fairly certain will never be received from the customer.

An irrecoverable debt will **reduce the cash flow** of a business, as it represents **income which it will no longer receive**.

 Definition

A **specific provision** for doubtful debts is a provision against a **particular** debt owed as there is concern than it may not be paid in full.

A **general provision** is a further provision consisting of normally a percentage of **remaining debts**. This reflects the fact that some debts may not be paid in full.

The specific and general provisions together form the doubtful debt provision which is credited in the statement of financial position against trade receivables, reducing the balance on the receivables.

This provision is an accounting entry only and **does not represent any reduction in the cash flow.** It is a prudent thing to do to make sure the accounts are as accurate as possible.

1.4 Administrative costs

If a company does not give credit then the sales system will often be very simple to operate and hence cheap. A business giving credit, by contrast, has more expensive recording and collection systems (as well as paying the wages of credit control staff), hence much **higher administrative expenses**.

2 Debt collection procedures

2.1 Administrative procedure

The collection of cash starts with the receipt of an **order**. The order is then agreed and processed. The business will deliver the goods and **send an invoice** detailing the payment amount and terms. It is helpful to file a **goods received note** in the credit management system as this helps credit controllers to substantiate claims of delivery. These notes must be diligently filed, having been signed by the recipient, dated and pre-numbered and matched with invoices. **Statements** should be sent out at the end of each period (usually monthly) detailing any outstanding balances.

If the terms of the credit agreement are being met then **payment** will be received and this will be recorded in the accounts of the business.

2.2 Debt collection policy

Some customers do not pay their invoices promptly and a **polite reminder** may be needed. Some customers may require more than a gentle reminder; it may be necessary to take legal action to obtain payment.

It is important to have a **planned approach** to non-payment problems to ensure that the company's cash flow is not severely affected.

Each company will have its own version of the debt collect policy; below is an example:

Debt collection process

- Invoices to be despatched on day of issue, (day of issue to be no more than 2 days after date of delivery).

- Statements to be despatched in the second week of the month.

- Aged trade receivable analysis to be produced and reviewed on a weekly basis.

- Reminder letter to be sent once an account is overdue.

- Telephone chaser for accounts 15 days overdue.

- Customer on stop list if no payment is received within 5 days of the telephone chaser. Computerised sales order processing system updated and automatic email sent to the customer contact and the account manager (sales person).

- Letter threatening legal action if payment not received within 30 days of the first letter.

- Legal proceedings/debt collection agency instructed subject to the approval of the Finance Director.

- Prepare a report suggesting an appropriate provision for irrecoverable or doubtful debts.

If at any stage in the process the customer is declared insolvent or bankrupt then contact the insolvency practitioner in order to register the debt and notify the financial accountant so that the VAT can be reclaimed.

The length of follow-up period will depend on whether the customer has merely overlooked payment or is trying to extend credit terms further.

In most cases, **with good credit control procedures, monies will be received** from credit customers, sometimes after encouragement such as reminder letters or telephone calls.

However, there will usually be some cases in which either the debt is never collected and has to be written off (irrecoverable debt), or the business has to resort to legal procedures to obtain payment.

Test your understanding 1

Put the following in a sensible order for a debt collection policy

A Send statement

B Irrecoverable debt

C Legal action letter

D Issue invoice

E Telephone call

F Customer on stop

G Provision for doubtful debt

H Reminder letter

I Start legal action

There are ways that a business can try to minimise the effect and, hopefully, incidences of non-payment or legal proceedings:

- Factoring
- Invoice discounting
- Credit insurance
- Restricting future trade
- Debt collection agencies
- Settlement discounts for prompt payment.

These are all covered later in this chapter and within chapter 4.

3 Credit control and the impact on cash flow and liquidity

3.1 Introduction

As discussed in the previous chapter, liquidity is the measure of how much cash, liquid assets or assets that are easily converted into cash a business has. The main sources of liquidity are usually:

- cash in the bank
- short term investments that can be cashed in easily and quickly
- cash inflows from normal trading operations (cash sales and payments by receivables for credit sales)
- an overdraft facility or other ready source of extra borrowing.

Adequate liquidity is often a key factor in contributing to the success or failure of a business. Inventory and receivables need to be turned into cash to enable businesses to pay their debts (payables) and other expenses.

Liquidity in the business means **having enough cash** or ready access to cash **to meet all payment obligations when these fall due**.

For many businesses, their entire revenue is made on credit terms and therefore it is critical to manage the process of granting credit in order to ensure that sales are only made to organisations that will pay to terms and that timely collection of these amounts is taken. Effective credit control is vital to a company's liquidity.

 Test your understanding 2

Why is liquidity important?

A   To ensure that a company does not make a loss

B   So that the shareholders can see how much return they will get on their investment

C   So that the company can estimate how much cash is tied up in inventory and non-current assets

D   So that the company can ensure that cash is available to discharge commitments

3.2   Impact of irrecoverable debts

It is possible that some debts will become irrecoverable debts i.e. the cash will not be received. The cash flows will need to be adjusted for this.

 Example

It has come to the attention of the credit control manager that one of the credit customers is going into liquidation. The customer bought £10,000 worth of goods in June. The credit manager has decided it is necessary to write off the outstanding amount as an irrecoverable debt.

The current credit sales budget is as follows:

	Actual			Forecast		
	April	May	June	July	August	September
Total sales	82,000	84,000	85,000	90,000	92,000	95,000

The pattern of sales receipts are 30% in the month of sale, 45% in the month following sale and 25% two months after sale.

	June	July	August	Sept
Original value of sales	85,000	90,000	92,000	95,000
30% in month of sale	25,500	27,000	27,600	28,500
45% in subsequent month	37,800	38,250	40,500	41,400
25% two months after sale	20,500	21,000	21,250	22,500
Original timing of receipts	83,800	86,250	89,350	92,400
Revised value of sales	75,000	90,000	92,000	95,000
30% in month of sale	**22,500**	27,000	27,600	28,500
45% in subsequent month	37,800	**33,750**	40,500	41,400
25% two months after sale	20,500	21,000	**18,750**	22,500
Revised timing of receipts	80,800	81,750	86,850	92,400
Change in receipts	–3,000	–4,500	–2,500	0

Note how the irrecoverable debt effects 3 months of the forecasted cash inflow due to the payment pattern of the receivables.

If a business sells VAT taxable goods or services to a customer, the VAT element is paid to HMRC. If the customer does not pay for the goods or services irrecoverable debt relief can be claimed.

For a business to be able to claim back the VAT that has been paid, the debt must:

- **be more than six months old and less than four years and six months old**

- **be written off**

- **not have been sold or handed to a factoring company**

- **not be more than the normal selling price for the items.**

Example

Iwerddon owes £27,000 (VAT inclusive) and is refusing to pay even though there is no dispute. The account is on stop. Attempts to contact the customer by letter and telephone have been unsuccessful. The debt is to be written off.

Required

Calculate how much VAT can be reclaimed?

Solution

27,000 ÷ 120 × 20 = 4,500

3.3 Impact of changes to credit terms

 Example

A cash budget has been prepared for Maximillian Ltd for the next 4 periods for a new product.

	March	April	May	June
Forecast sales revenue £	15,600	18,000	20,400	22,800

The pattern of cash receipts used in the budget assumed 50% of sales were received in the month of sale and the remaining 50% in the month following sale.

	March	April	May	June
Original forecast sales receipts £	7,800	16,800	19,200	21,600

In the light of current economic trends Maximillian Ltd needs to adjust its cash budget to take account of the following:

- The pattern of sales receipts will change to 25% of sales received in the month of sale, 30% in the month following sale and the remaining 45% two months after sale.

Required

What will be the impact of the change in credit terms on the cash receipts?

Solution

	Sales receipts				
	March £	April £	May £	June £	Total £
March sales	3,900	4,680	7,020	0	
April sales	0	4,500	5,400	8,100	
May sales	0	0	5,100	6,120	
June sales	0	0	0	5,700	
Revised forecast sales receipts	3,900	9,180	17,520	19,920	50,520

Receipts from sales in March to June will decrease by 22.8% if the timing of receipts changes.

4 Settlement discounts

4.1 Cash or settlement discounts

With some credit agreements there will be a **discount offered** as an **incentive** to pay the money owed within a **certain time frame**.

For example, the normal credit period may be 90 days, but the business may be prepared to offer a 1% discount for payment within 45 days. This discount would be described as '1/45, net 90'.

The costs and benefits of a cash discount scheme are summarised below:

Benefits

- Reduction in finance charges

- Reduction in irrecoverable debts due to reduced collection period

- Improved customer relations and potential extra sales

- Improves short term liquidity as cash received sooner

Costs

- Cost of discount (reduced revenue received)

- Extra administrative costs

- Potential abuse of scheme (customer takes discount but does not pay early)

4.2 Impact of discounts on liquidity and cash flow

The payment pattern of receivables will be altered by offering settlement discounts (prompt payment discounts) to credit customers. Settlement discounts should encourage earlier payment of debts as customers who pay earlier pay less.

 Example

A business is considering whether to offer a 3% discount for payment received from credit customers in the month of sale. This will only be offered to sales made after 1 April.

Credit sales for the business are as follows:

	Actual		Budgeted		
	February £	March £	April £	May £	June £
Credit sales	20,000	22,000	24,000	18,000	21,000

The current receivables collection forecast is:

- 15% in month of sale

- 75% in month after sale

- 10% two months after sale

	April £	May £	June £
Original forecast sales receipts	22,100	22,900	19,050

The business estimates that 60% of customers would take advantage of the settlement discount by paying in the month of sale, 30% of customers will pay in the month after the sale and 10% of customers will pay two months after the month of sale.

Required

Should this business offer a settlement discount?

Solution

	April £	May £	June £
Cash from receivables in month of sale (£ × 60% × 97%)	13,968	10,476	12,222
Cash from receivables in month after sale	22,000 × 75% = 16,500	24,000 × 30% = 7,200	18,000 × 30% = 5,400
Cash from receivables in two months after month of sale (£ × 10%)	2,000	2,200	2,400
Total receipts	32,468	19,876	20,022

This business should offer a settlement discount of 3% as cash receipts have increased by 13% over the 3 months in question.

Original total receipts £64,050

New total receipts £72,366

4.3 Assessing the cost of a discount policy

There are two calculations that are used to assess the **annual equivalent cost** of offering a discount either using simple interest or compound interest.

The simple annual cost of offering a discount to trade receivables is calculated by using this formula:

$$\frac{d}{100 - d} \times \frac{365}{N - D} \times 100$$

Where: d = discount percentage given

N = normal payment term

D = discount payment term

Example – simple annual cost

Current credit terms are payment within 60 days. The finance director is considering introducing a settlement discount of 3% for payments received in the month that the sales invoice is raised (within 30 days).

Calculate the simple annual cost of the proposed discount.

$$\text{Annual cost} = \frac{d}{100-d} \times \frac{365}{N-D} \times 100$$

$$= \frac{3}{100-3} \times \frac{365}{60-30} \times 100 = 37.6\%$$

As it would cost 37.6% per annum to offer this discount, it would almost certainly be cheaper to borrow from the bank to raise any funds required.

The compound annual cost of offering a discount to trade receivables is calculated by using this formula:

$$[(1 + \frac{d}{100-d}) \wedge (\frac{365}{N-D})] -1 \times 100$$

Where: d = discount percentage given

N = normal payment term

D = discount payment term

^ = to the power of

 Example – Compound annual cost

Current credit terms are payment within 60 days. The finance director is considering introducing a settlement discount of 3% for payments received in the month that the sales invoice is raised (within 30 days).

Calculate the compound annual cost of the proposed discount.

$$\text{Annual cost} = (1 + \frac{d}{100-d}) \wedge (\frac{365}{N-D}) -1 \times 100$$

$$\text{Annual cost} = (1 + \frac{3}{100-3}) \wedge (\frac{365}{60-30}) -1 \times 100$$

$$= 1.03093 \wedge 12.167 - 1 \times 100$$

$$= 44.86\%$$

As it would cost 44.86% per annum to offer this discount, it would almost certainly be cheaper to borrow from the bank to raise any funds required.

Test your understanding 3

What is the simple annual cost of giving a 5% prompt payment discount to customers who pay within 30 days rather than the usual 90 days?

A   21%

B   64%

C   32%

D   3.1%

 Test your understanding 4

A company is concerned about the size of its trade receivables and its cash flows. It therefore decides to offer a 'prompt payment discount' of 1.5% for payment within 14 days. Without the discount, customers take 60 days' credit.

What is the compound annual interest rate of the discount?

A   12.7%

B   39.1%

C   0.2%

D   39.7%

 Test your understanding 5

A company is concerned about the size of its trade receivables and its cash flows. It therefore decides to offer a 'prompt payment discount' of 3% for payment within 10 days. Without the discount, customers take 45 days' credit.

What is the simple annual interest rate of the discount?

A   112.9%

B   18.8%

C   32.3%

D   310.0%

5 Factoring

5.1 Factoring arrangements

 Definition

Factoring involves the use of a factoring company to provide sales ledger services, finance and in some cases protection against irrecoverable debts in return for a fee.

A company may wish to outsource the collection of its debts through a factoring arrangement. This relieves the company of the burden of maintaining a detailed credit control system.

A factoring arrangement can be taken out with a factoring company (the 'factor'). Factoring companies are generally controlled by the clearing banks which gives considerable credence to the industry.

5.2 Options available

The factoring arrangement usually allows for the following.

(a) **Administration of the sales ledger and credit control functions**. The factor takes on the function of the credit control team. The factor will issue credit approval, chase debts and collect the cash.

This facility only leaves the client the work of raising invoices and clearing disputes, as the factoring company effectively runs the sales ledger. The client has little need for a sophisticated computer system; the cost of such a scheme is between 0.75% and 3% of revenue.

(b) **Finance**. If the company requires cash immediately, the factoring company may provide up to 85% of the value of the debt immediately. This is effectively a cash advance and usually costs slightly more than bank borrowing rates. However, the payment is certain and allows for a determined cash flow.

(c) **Credit protection**. This can be provided by the factor to cover against irrecoverable debts.

Definition

If the factoring agreement is 'without recourse' then the factor bears the risk of any trade receivables that do not pay.

If the agreement is 'with recourse' then the customer will have to repay to the factor any monies advanced for the debt that is irrecoverable.

'Without recourse' is more expensive as the risk for the factor is higher.

5.3   The debt factoring procedure

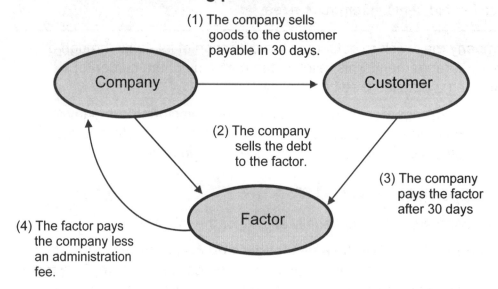

(1) The company sells goods to the customer payable in 30 days.

Company → Customer

(2) The company sells the debt to the factor.

(3) The company pays the factor after 30 days

Factor

(4) The factor pays the company less an administration fee.

1   An invoice is raised as normal to the customer but at the same time the invoice/debt is sold to a Factor.

2   If the Factoring arrangement is being used to improve cash flow the Factor gives you up to 85% of the amount owing when the invoice is raised. If factoring is only being used to administer the credit control department this step is missed out.

3   The factoring company will make a charge for this service and then run the ledger and chase up the debts.

4   The balance on the debt is paid once the customer has settled with the Factor.

5.4   Advantages of debt factoring

Factoring is particularly useful in the early stages of development when a company is sufficiently large to need to devote attention to trade receivables but not yet large enough to warrant employing a full-time credit manager.

The advantages of debt factoring are as follows:

- The company need **no longer incur the costs** of employing its own credit control staff.

- Because the factor can act for several companies concurrently, the client will benefit from the **economies of scale** of such an organisation and the factor's fees are reduced.

- The **cash flow advantages** that ensue from a regular predetermined cash inflow should reduce the company's financing charges thereby improving liquidity.

5.5   Disadvantages of debt factoring

The main disadvantages of factoring are that:

- Control of trade receivables is surrendered to the factor, which may **displease customers**.

- Factoring may give the impression to suppliers and customers that the company is having liquidity problems.

6 Invoice discounting

6.1 Invoice discounting

Invoice discounting is the purchase of invoices from a company, but, unlike debt factoring, the **invoice discounter does not take over control of debt collection**. The invoice discounter solely supplies an advance of cash.

6.2 The invoice discounting procedure

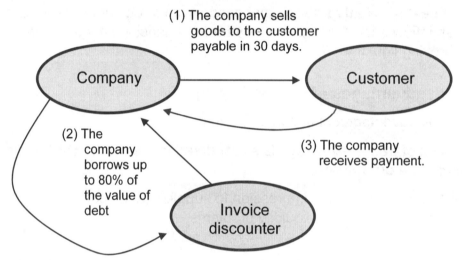

1   The company sends out invoices, statements and reminders in the normal way.

2   The invoice discounter provides cash to the company for a proportion of the value of the invoice, once it has received a copy of the invoice and agreed to discount it. The discounter will advance cash up to 80% of face value.

3   The company then chases and collects the debts due from the customer.

4   When the company collects the payment from its customer, the money must be paid into a bank account controlled by the invoice discounter. The invoice discounter then pays the business the remainder of the invoice, less interest and administration charges.

Invoice discounting does not need to apply to the whole sales ledger and can be negotiated piecemeal for particular selections of invoices. When a batch of debts is assigned, the discounting company will advance up to 80% of the gross invoice value.

The invoice discounter relies on the credit control procedures of the business to get their money repaid. Therefore this service may only be available to well established businesses. The customer does not need to know of the invoice discounting arrangement.

6.3 Advantages of invoice discounting

- Simple and flexible.

- Can be used when short term funds are needed – improving liquidity.

- The customer does not need to know of the invoice discounting arrangement.

6.4 Disadvantages of invoice discounting

- The main disadvantage of invoice discounting is the discounter's fees.

 Test your understanding 6

Invoice discounting is:

A   A reduced price for goods

B   A reduced price for early payment

C   A finance house lending money against invoices issued

D   A judgement by court

Test your understanding 7

Bogstandard Brooms Ltd has been experiencing difficulty in collecting its debts within the terms of 30 days which they offer. Its sales ledger balances total, on average, £500,000 which is equivalent to 60 days sales. The company has an overdraft facility of £750,000 on which it pays interest of 8% per annum. Because of the high level of receivables, the overdraft level is never less than £500,000.

Cashrich Credit plc have offered them a without recourse factoring arrangement whereby they will administer the sales ledger, pay 85% of the invoice value immediately it is issued and the balance when they are paid by the customer or 60 days later, whichever is the earlier. They will charge 2½% of the revenue which is estimated at £3,000,000 per annum.

You estimate that this will save administration costs of the sales ledger of £15,000 per annum. Assuming that the customers will still pay after 60 days, will this be cost effective or not? Show your calculations.

 Test your understanding 8

A company has monthly credit sales of £200,000 and it gives customers 60 days credit. All customers take the full credit allowed. It has irrecoverable debts each year amounting to about 2.5% of revenue. It operates with a bank overdraft and pays interest at 8% on its overdraft balance.

The company's management is considering whether to use a factor to collect its debts, under a non-recourse factoring arrangement. A factor has indicated that it will take over the administration of the sales ledger and debt collection for a fee of 2% of annual credit sales revenue. This would save the company internal operating costs of £30,000 each year.

The factor would also charge 1.5% of revenue for credit insurance. The factor will advance 80% of the value of invoices as soon as they are sent out, and charge interest at 7.75%. If the services of the factor are used, it is anticipated that there will be no change in annual sales revenue and no change in the collection period of 60 days.

Required

Assess the financial consequences of using the factor for non-recourse factoring and factor finance.

7 Credit insurance

7.1 Credit insurance

Credit insurance is a method of **guarding against unexpected failures**. Credit management is still required but it is a way of safeguarding the cash flow. It may be particularly useful when a company deals with one or two major customers and is therefore dependent upon them.

Credit insurance is obtained through a broker who establishes terms and an agreement between the insured and the underwriter. The broker receives a commission for his, her or their work and, if he, she or they negotiates the policy well, will be able to renew it in the following year.

The types of cover available fall into four main categories:

(a) whole revenue – covers all irrecoverable debts

(b) datum line – only customers with debts over a certain limit are insured

(c) catastrophe – only insured once an agreed level of irrecoverable debt has been incurred

(d) specific account – only certain particular customers are insured.

The amount that is usually claimed for is the **net** amount as VAT can be reclaimed from HMRC.

7.2 Selecting the correct policy

Each company will have its own system of credit control and its own pattern of sales/trade receivables. Entire revenue policies are available to cover all possible irrecoverable debts, usually with a de minimis limit, but these are often very expensive. A more specific policy can be taken out, such as a datum line policy, which covers customers whose indebtedness exceeds an agreed amount.

Alternatively, a policy-holder may decide to exclude certain large customers in whom he, she or they has full confidence, and so the policy becomes quite specific in its nature with only certain individual accounts insured.

7.3 Terms of the policy

Most policies insure between 75% and 90% of agreed sales. The premium is negotiable between the parties.

A credit limit will need to be agreed for each customer. This is sometimes a difficult part to negotiate as the insured may well require a higher level of credit to cover the expected trade with the customer than the underwriter is prepared to accept. Trading above the agreed limit may invalidate the policy; but having to restrict sales to the customer may lose goodwill. A good relationship with the underwriter may help to solve this problem.

7.4 Catastrophe policies

The main features of catastrophe policies are as follows:

(a) the insured agrees to bear the first £1,000, say, of the loss due to the catastrophe

(b) above this aggregate limit the cover will reimburse a specified percentage of the loss

(c) this policy is not normally suitable for small companies.

Credit insurance is a means of **protecting against irrecoverable debts**; however, it is usually a **costly** way of obtaining security and many companies may decide to bear the cost of irrecoverable debts themselves when they are confident that this is less expensive than the insurance premium.

 Test your understanding 9

Reign Ltd owes a balance of £48,000 including VAT. The account is on stop. Attempts to contact the customer by telephone and letter have been unsuccessful. The account is credit insured but only 75% of the value of debt is insured.

Complete the sentence:

Contact the credit insurer to make a claim for £_____, make a provision for £ _____ and claim VAT of £_____ from HMRC.

8 Summary

There are a variety of methods for collection of debts which may help businesses in different circumstances.

Early settlement discounts can help liquidity in the short term by encouraging customers to pay early, but can be expensive in the longer term.

Factoring arrangements can relieve a business of having to collect its own debts and can also be useful for cash flow purposes if funds are advanced and the debts are collected by the factor.

Invoice discounting also allows money to be advanced to the business but still the business has the job of collecting their debts.

Debt insurance is a way of guarding against the non-payment of debts but is often a fairly expensive option.

Test your understanding answers

 ### Test your understanding 1

Put the following in a sensible order for a debt collection policy

D   Issue invoice

A   Send statement

E   Telephone call

H   Reminder letter

F   Customer on stop

C   Legal action letter

G   Provision for doubtful debt

I   Start legal action

B   Irrecoverable debt

There are alternatives that would also be considered sensible e.g. the reminder letter may be sent before the telephone call is made, the provision for doubtful debt may be provided earlier in the process.

 ### Test your understanding 2

Answer D

 ### Test your understanding 3

Answer C

The supplier gains 60 days' use of the amount due at a cost of 5%, i.e. an annual rate of:

$(5/(100 - 5)) \times (365/(90 - 30)) \times 100 = 32\%$.

This discount rate is unlikely to be worthwhile in the UK.

Test your understanding 4

Answer A

$\{[(1 + 1.5/98.5) \wedge (365/(60 - 14))] - 1\} \times 100 = 12.7\%$

 Test your understanding 5

Answer C

$(3/97) \times (365/(45 - 10)) \times 100 = 32.3\%$

 Test your understanding 6

Answer C

 Test your understanding 7

Currently the company is incurring two costs that could be saved if they accepted the without recourse facility offered by Cashrich Credit plc.

Savings

Admin costs of sales ledger	£15,000
Interest – 8% of £500,000 × 85%	£34,000
	£49,000

Costs

Charges £3,000,000 × 2½%	£75,000

As the costs exceed the savings, it would not be in the company's interest to accept the facility.

Test your understanding 8

		Costs of factoring £	Savings £
Sales ledger administration	2% × £200,000 × 12	48,000	
Administration cost savings			30,000
Credit protection insurance	1.5% × £200,000 × 12	36,000	
Reduction in bad debt losses	2.5% × £200,000 × 12		60,000
Cost of factor finance	7.75% × 80% × £200,000 × 2 months	24,800	
Overdraft interest saved	8% × 80% × £200,000 × 2 months		25,600
Total		108,800	115,600
Net benefit from factoring	(115,600 – 108,800)		6,800

Test your understanding 9

Contact the credit insurer to make a claim for (£48,000 ÷ 120 × 100) × 75% = £30,000, make a provision for (£48,000 ÷ 120 × 100) × 25% = £10,000 and claim VAT of £48,000 ÷ 120 × 20 = £8,000 from HMRC.

Managing trade receivables

Introduction

In this chapter, we will consider how it is best to monitor the trade receivables of a business, and how to manage late payers and potential non-payers.

ASSESSMENT CRITERIA	CONTENTS
Communicate with stakeholders using a professional and ethical approach (3.4) Legal and administrative procedures for debt collection (4.1) Insolvency (4.2)	1 Monitoring debt collection 2 Restricting future trade 3 Debt collection agencies 4 Court procedures 5 Bankruptcy and liquidation 6 Communication with trade receivables

1 Monitoring debt collection

1.1 Introduction

If a credit customer of a business goes into liquidation it is highly unlikely that the business will receive the cash owed. This will negatively impact the cash flow of the business. Careful monitoring of credit customers is required to reduce the risk of this occurring.

The credit manager should closely monitor the collection of debts. Since this is of such fundamental importance to the cash flow, it is a regular if not daily task. It is important for all the departments in the company to pool their collective knowledge.

The credit manager needs to be looking for:

(a)   customers who are building up a significant outstanding account

(b)   customers who have not paid for a long period of time

(c)   customers whose cheques have been dishonoured by their bank.

Any indication of the above should warn the credit manager that the customer may be having problems and he, she or they should warn the sales department to be wary of making any more sales to these customers.

1.2 Analysis of the aged trade receivables listing

The regular review of the aged trade receivable analysis should highlight the following potential problems:

*   credit limit exceeded

*   slow payers

*   recent debts cleared but older outstanding amount

*   old amounts outstanding and no current trading.

Each of these will be considered in turn.

1.3 Credit limit exceeded

If a customer's account balance shows that their credit limit has been exceeded then this must be investigated.

This is sometimes due to a **lack of communication** between the sales department and the sales ledger department. However, before a new sale on credit is agreed with a credit customer, it should be standard practice to ensure that this new sale will not mean that the customer has exceeded the agreed credit limit.

If a customer is highlighted in the aged trade receivable listing as having exceeded their credit limit then normally the customer should be told that **no further sales** will be made to them until at least some of the outstanding balances have been repaid.

However, in some circumstances, liaison between the sales ledger and the sales department may result in an **increase in the customer's credit limit** if they have a good payment record and are simply increasing their trade with us rather than just delaying payment of the amounts due.

1.4 Slow payers

Some businesses can be identified from the aged trade receivable listing as being slow payers as they always have amounts **outstanding for, say, 31 to 60 days and 61 to 90 days as well as current amounts**. In these cases consideration should be given to methods of encouraging the customer to pay earlier. This could be in the form of a letter from the finance director or perhaps more successfully the offer of a settlement discount for earlier payment.

1.5 Recent debts cleared but older outstanding amount

If a customer is generally a regular payer and the most recent debts have been cleared but there is still an outstanding older amount then this will normally indicate either a **query over the amount outstanding** or a problem with the recording of invoices, credit notes or payments received.

1.6 Old amounts outstanding and no current trading

This is probably the most concerning situation for a credit manager. In this case it would appear that the **trade receivable is no longer buying from the business** but still owes money from previous purchases. In this case, the trade receivable should be contacted immediately and payment sought. If no contact can be made with the trade receivable or there is a genuine problem with payment, such as bankruptcy or liquidation, consideration should be given to writing off the debt as irrecoverable.

Specific provision for doubtful debts

As soon as there is a problem with a trade receivable which indicates they may be unable to pay a debt, it is **prudent to provide against the debt**. A specific provision can be set up for debts and a list is compiled of:

(a) invoices disputed

(b) invoices with warranty claims

(c) part-payment invoices

(d) old invoices

(e) suspense account items.

The total figure forms part of the specific provision and is written off against the year's profit.

Assessing irrecoverable debts

The credit controller is in a position to be able to assess potential irrecoverable debts. Information used to do this might include the following:

- evidence of long outstanding debts from the aged trade receivables analysis

- a one-off outstanding debt when more recent debts have been cleared

- correspondence with trade receivables

- outstanding older debts and no current business with the customer

- press comment

- information from the sales team.

Communicating potential irrecoverable debts

This will normally be the decision of a senior person in the accounting function. Therefore, if there is information about potential irrecoverable or doubtful debts then all of this information should be communicated clearly to the relevant person within the accounting function.

Incidence of irrecoverable debts

It can be argued that a high level of irrecoverable debts in an organisation is an indicator of poor credit control, although there could obviously be other reasons such as the general economic climate. A high level of irrecoverable debts could be an indication of:

- sales being made to high risk customers

- poor assessment of creditworthiness

- lack of useful information for checking on creditworthiness

- weak sales ledger accounting

- poor follow up procedures for outstanding debts.

1.7   80/20 rule

Analysis of trade receivables can be simplified using the **Pareto's Principle** or the **80/20 rule**. Vilfredo Pareto noted that 20% of the people in Italy owned 80% of the country's wealth.

If this principle is applied to the trade receivables of a company it could help the credit manager focus the credit control team. The credit manager could assume that 80% of the debts owed in value were due to only 20% of the customer accounts thereby focusing attention and analysis on these 20% of customers.

1.8 Materiality

Another way to assess trade receivables is on the materiality of the debt or the value of debt in comparison to total value of trade receivables. If one debt is the majority of the trade receivables then attention needs to be focused on receiving that money.

The credit manager also needs to consider the cost of collecting the debt in comparison to the value of the debt. A small outstanding amount may cost more to collect than it is actually worth to the business.

Example

Wood Limited

Trade receivables' age analysis at 31.12.X1

Account no	Name	Credit limit £	Total £	Up to 30 days £	31–60 days £	61–90 days £	Over 90 days £
A001	ABC Limited	10,000	9,580	9,500	–	80	–
A002	DEF Limited	20,000	400	400	–	–	–
A003	GHI Limited	15,000	14,000	10,000	3,000	1,000	–
A004	JKL Limited	2,500	2,500	–	–	2,000	500
A005	MNO Limited	3,500	4,000	1,500	2,500	–	–
Total			30,480	21,400	5,500	3,080	500
%			100	70.2	18.0	10.2	1.6

Solution

Taking each trade receivable in turn we will consider what information the aged debt analysis has provided and what further action might be taken.

ABC Ltd   The vast majority of this debt is current therefore there may be some dispute over the £80 over 60 days old which should be investigated.

DEF Ltd   There would appear to be no problems with this account.

GHI Ltd   This would appear to be a slow payer and encouragement should be given to pay the older debts.

JKL Ltd   This trade receivable is a concern. There has been no trading with this customer in the last two months and their full credit limit has been used and is still outstanding after 61 and 90 days.

MNO Ltd   This trade receivable has been allowed to exceed the credit limit set by £500. The reason for this should be investigated and either supplies should be stopped until some of the outstanding balance has been cleared or the credit limit should be reassessed.

The percentage of each ageing of total trade receivables is also useful information for the credit manager as any increase in the older trade receivables percentage would be a cause for concern.

Test your understanding 1

Jones Limited has sold goods on credit to Smith plc. The following information is available.

(i)   Aged trade receivable analysis

(ii)   Copies of outstanding invoices

(iii)   Copies of trade references

(iv)   Copies of contractual documents

(v)   Copies of bank references

Which of the above will be needed to aid collection of the debts from Smith plc?

A   All items

B   (i), (ii) and (iii) only

C   (i), (ii) and (iv) only

D   (iii) and (v) only

1.9   Updating the aged trade receivable analysis

The aged trade receivable analysis can be prepared by updating the previous analysis for any invoices issued in the period and any cash received in the period.

The monthly balance, if still remaining unpaid, must then move into the column representing one month further outstanding.

For example, if an invoice in the 'up to 30 days' column is not paid in the following month then it moves into the '31 to 60 days' column.

Example

Given below is an extract from the aged trade receivable analysis for a company at 30 April 20X4

Account	Name	Credit limit £	Total £	Up to 30 days £	31 – 60 days £	61 – 90 days £	> 90 days £
0001	Ace Partners	6,000	4,800	2,100 inv 0257	1,700 inv 0244	1,000 inv 0211	
0002	Aflek Ltd	10,000	8,850	4,550 inv 0259	4,000 inv 0247		300 inv 0196
0003	Amber Ltd	5,000	2,400	2,400 inv 0252			

During the month of May 20X4 the following transactions took place with these trade receivables:

Ace Partners	Invoice 0269 issued for £1,800
Paid invoice	0211
Aflek Ltd	Invoice 0266 issued for £1,300
	Paid half of invoice 0247
Amber Ltd	Invoice 0273 issued for £2,200

Update the aged trade receivable analysis to reflect the transactions in May 20X4.

Solution

Account	Name	Credit limit £	Total £	Up to 30 days £	31 – 60 days £	61 – 90 days £	> 90 days £
0001	Ace Partners	6,000	5,600	1,800 inv 0269	2,100 inv 0257	1,700 inv 0244	
0002	Aflek Ltd	10,000	8,150	1,300 inv 0266	4,550 inv 0259	2,000 inv 0247	300 inv 0196
0003	Amber Ltd	5,000	4,600	2,200 inv 0273	2,400 inv 0252		

Test your understanding 2

You are working in Wilson Limited's credit control section. The Sales Manager has asked for your views on the credit status of four organisations to whom Wilson Limited supplies goods.

Customer name and address	Total due £	Current month £	Up to 30 days £	Up to 60 days £	Up to 90 days £	Over 90 days £
Megacorp plc	72,540	10,000	11,250	12,250	15,500	23,540
Credit limit £85,000						Terms of sale: 60 days net
Goodfellows Cycles	24,000	9,500	9,500			5,000
Credit limit £50,000						Terms of sale: 30 days net
Hooper-bikes	26,750	5,000	6,250	4,875	5,275	5,350
Credit limit £25,000						Terms of sale: 60 days net
Dynamo Cycles	7,250	4,500	2,750			
Credit limit £7,500						Terms of sale: 30 days net

Using the extracts from the aged analysis of trade receivables given above, analyse these four accounts and write a memorandum to the Sales Manager.

Your memorandum should:

- provide an opinion of the creditworthiness of the customer and the status of the account

- suggest how the account should be managed in future.

MEMORANDUM

To: Sales Manager

Date: XX-XX-XX

From: Credit controller

Subject: Credit status of organisations

Test your understanding 3

Debt collection policy for Purple Ltd is as follows:

(i)   Invoices are issued at time of delivery.

(ii)   Terms are payment within 30 days.

(iii)   Aged analysis is produced monthly.

(iv)   Reminder telephone call is made when the debt is 7 days overdue.

(v)   Overdue letter is sent when debt is 14 days overdue.

(vi)   At 28 days overdue the account is put on stop.

(vii) At 60 days overdue it is placed in hands of debt collector unless debt is disputed or legal proceedings are started.

(viii) Purple Ltd is credit insured, however insurance is only given for customers once they have a history of trade with the business of at least 12 months and have successfully paid at least 2 invoiced amounts.

Aged analysis of trade receivables at 31 October 2010

Customer	Balance £	Current £	31 – 60 days £	61 – 90 days £	Over 90 days £
Orange Ltd	40,000				40,000
Yellow Ltd	22,500		22,500		
Red Ltd	50,000			24,000	26,000

Notes

- Orange Ltd is a new customer and has said that the goods were not received in good condition. The delivery note states that any claim for poor quality goods has to be notified to Purple Ltd within 24 hours.

  Orange Ltd only raised a problem with the goods when they were called for a second time. They did not mention that the goods were poor quality on the first call or within 24 hours of delivery.

- Yellow Ltd is a regular customer and usually pays to terms.

- Red Ltd is refusing to pay even though there is no dispute.

KAPLAN PUBLISHING

For each of the above, state what action should have been taken to date and what further action will need to be taken. State whether any provision should be made in each case.

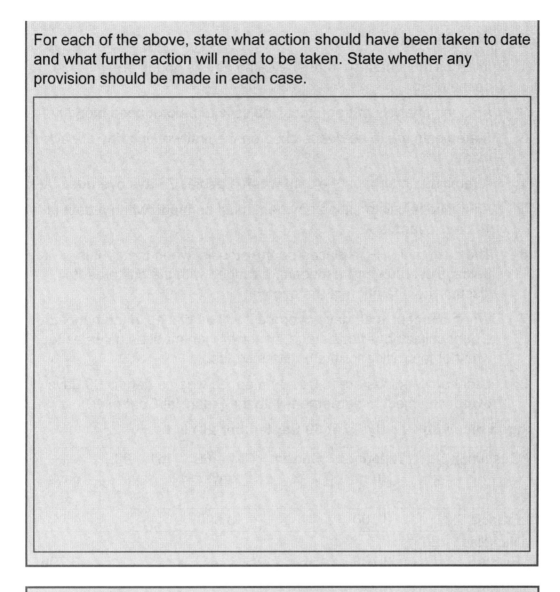

Test your understanding 4

You work for Henry Tudor. The policy for the collection of debts, an extract from the aged receivables analysis and supporting customer notes are set out below. You should assume that today's date is 1 October 20Y0. On the basis of this information, write a memo to Henry Tudor. Your memo should include:

1   In the case of Francis Ltd, a note of the matters to be discussed by telephone.

2   In the case of Nicholas Evans, who is a sole trader, a description of two methods which may be used to enforce judgement.

3   The credit control action required for each of the other accounts.

Debt collection policy

1 Invoices must be issued on the same day as goods are despatched.

2 An aged analysis of trade receivables is to be produced monthly.

3 Statements are to be despatched on the first working day of each month.

4 A reminder letter must be sent when a debt is 7 days overdue.

5 A telephone call to chase payment must be made when a debt is 14 days overdue.

6 The customer will be placed on the stop list when the debt is 30 days overdue and a meeting arranged with the customer to discuss the operation of the account.

7 When the debt is 45 days overdue it will be placed in the hands of a debt collector. At this stage, consideration must be given as to whether to provide for the outstanding debt.

8 Legal proceedings are to be commenced when a debt is 90 days overdue subject to agreement with the Financial Controller.

Aged receivable analysis at 30 September 20Y0

Customer	Amount due £	Current £	31 – 60 days £	61 – 90 days £	91+ days £
Francis Ltd	8,500		8,500		
Nicholas Evans	3,700				3,700
Shields Ltd	1,300	550		750	
Outdoors Ltd	850			850	

Notes

1 All four accounts were offered 30 day credit terms.

2 There are two outstanding invoices from Francis Ltd, both dated 16 August 20Y0.

3 A county court judgement has been obtained against Nicholas Evans.

4 There is an outstanding invoice from Shields Ltd for £750 dated 25 July 20Y0.

5 The amount due from Outdoors Ltd relates to an invoice dated 5 July 20Y0.

Memorandum

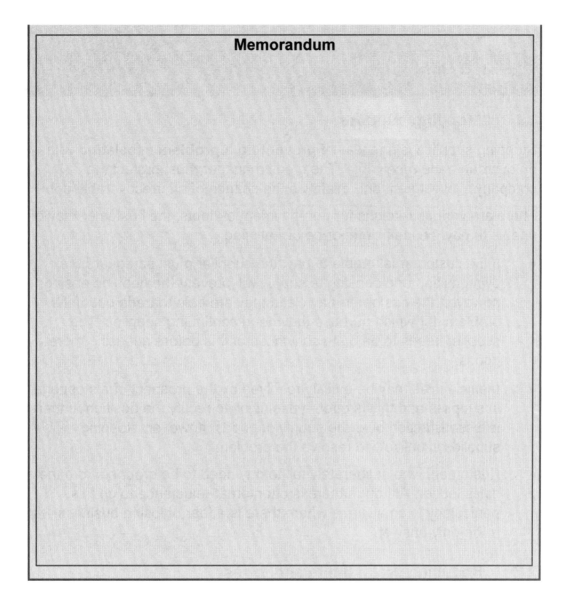

2 Restricting future trade

2.1 Stopping supplies

Stopping supplies is one way of **preventing a problem escalating** with an overdue trade receivable. The credit manager must protect the company's investment and minimise the chance of an irrecoverable debt.

There are various reasons for non-payment of debts: the customer may be unable to pay, be inefficient, or be dissatisfied.

- If the customer is unable to pay, the supplier must safeguard their own position and ceasing to supply will prevent the debt increasing; however, the customer may claim they are able to trade out of the problem, for which purpose they need continuing supplies. The supplier needs to be quite convinced of this before releasing more goods.

- Inefficiencies may be quickly resolved by the prospect of a stoppage in supplies and this is often a useful jolt to rectify the position. If there is dissatisfaction over the supply of goods, however, stopping supplies is unlikely to resolve the problem.

- Customers who deliberately fail to pay need to be dropped from the sales ledger. Although there is often great reluctance to do this – particularly in small firms where there is a fear of losing business – it is the only answer.

2.2 Reducing credit limits and terms

The credit controller may wish to reduce the amount of credit a company can have and/or the length of time the credit balance is allowed to remain outstanding. This should then reduce the risk and enable the credit control team to take action before the issue becomes too serious.

3 Debt collection agencies

3.1 Debt collection agencies

A collection agency can be appointed to collect debts. Various types of agency exist but they can generally be split into three types:

(a) **trade associations** are usually non-profit making bodies who charge an annual membership fee and a percentage of the monies recovered

(b) **voucher agencies** sell books of collection vouchers to client companies who are entitled to complete a voucher for any outstanding debt and send it to the agency

(c) **commercial agencies** usually work on a 'no-collection, no-charge' basis.

Collection agencies have the advantage of relieving the credit manager of the time-consuming work of chasing customers. A good agency will be specialised in tracing trade receivables that have disappeared, and will often have legal expertise. The charge is reasonable compared with the cost of employing another member of staff. It is important to remember that debt collection agencies have **no special legal powers** to collect the debts.

However, if the credit manager has efficient staff they may be able to do the work and so save the costs of an agency. Customers rarely respond well to outside agencies whose sole aim is to obtain payment of a debt and **goodwill can easily be lost** by such steps. If a customer is regularly defaulting on payment then debt collection agencies can have more of an impact on the customer.

It is usually sensible to check that the agency:

(a) is of good standing in the locality

(b) is licensed for debt collection under the Consumer Credit Act 1974 and 2006

(c) is financially sound

(d) uses an audited client trust account with its bank

(e) reports regularly to the company and returns payments promptly.

> ### ◖ Test your understanding 5
>
> Debt collection agencies are used because:
>
> A   They have extra powers to collect debts
>
> B   They can stop other companies supplying goods to the trade receivable with the outstanding debt
>
> C   They have the right to take goods from the trade receivable
>
> D   Customers take more notice of them and are therefore more likely to pay

4   Court procedures

4.1   How to bring a dispute to court

If it is necessary to take legal action against a receivable who has not paid then the initial step is to instruct a solicitor. The solicitor will require the following:

- details of the goods or services provided

- the date the liability arose

- the exact name and trading status of the receivable

- any background information such as disputes in the past

- copies of any invoices that are unpaid.

In some cases, there may be a negotiated settlement between the payable (money owed to) and receivable (money owed by) as the receivable does not want to run the risk of going to court. However, in other situations the case will be taken to court.

4.2   Appropriate courts

Outstanding amounts owed to an entity are **civil claims**. The route the case follows is decided by the judge and is based on the value of the claim and how complicated the case is. There are three routes or tracks:

- Less complicated and lower value claims (**up to £10,000**) will be dealt with by the <u>**Small Claims Track**</u>.

- Claims **between £10,000 and £25,000** that are capable of being tried within one day are allocated to the **Fast Track**.

- Claims **over £25,000** or more **complex cases** that will require more than one day in court are allocated to the **Multi Track** route.

These tracks are labels for the use of the court system not separate courts. A judge will decide if the case will be dealt with in a fast track or multi-track hearing once the claimant and the defendant have filed initial paperwork.

Note: the **County Court** deals with all cases allocated to the small claims track, the majority of the fast track and some multi track cases. All other claims are dealt with by the **High Court**.

4.3 Procedure

The appropriate court, once it has received all of the paperwork will issue a summons to the receivable requiring an acknowledgement of service of the summons. If the receivable does not reply then the judgement will go against them.

The receivable may admit the claim and perhaps offer to pay by instalments. If the payable does not accept this, then the court will determine a suitable method of paying off the debt.

 Test your understanding 6

If an outstanding debt is more than £5,000 the court that would deal with any action would be:

A   The high court

B   An industrial tribunal

C   A small claims court

D   The county court

4.4 Enforcing a court judgement

Once the court order has been made then the money must be collected and there are a number of methods of achieving this.

(a) **Garnishee order**

A garnishee order allows the payable to be paid directly by a receivable of the offending company i.e. a third party who also owes the defaulting company money.

(b) **Warrant of execution**

Seizing goods is effective against businesses with valuable items in their offices, such as computers. The court bailiff is given a 'warrant of execution'. The bailiff will seize the goods and sell them by public auction with the proceeds paid to the payable.

(c) **Warrant of delivery**

A warrant of delivery is used by the bailiff to reclaim the specific goods that the outstanding debt is related to and return the goods to the lawful owner.

(d) **Attachment of earnings order**

An attachment of earnings order ensures that the payable is paid directly by the receivable's employer out of his/her/their pay packet.

This is only available against individual receivables who are in employment and is usually very unsuccessful as the court needs to determine the 'protected' earnings of the individual and the receivable's employer needs to co-operate fully. Such a person is likely to change employment frequently, which creates further complications in tracing them and taking out fresh attachment orders.

(e) **Administrative order**

Where a receivable has a number of debts totalling less than £5,000 then the receivable might make regular payments into court and the court distributes them to the payables on a pro rata basis.

(f) **Charging order**

The court can order a charge on the receivable's property and if the debt is not paid within six months, the payable has the right to have the property sold.

(g) **Bankruptcy notice** (against a partner or individual)

A bankruptcy notice is usually very effective as few people like to go out of business. For a bankruptcy order to succeed the debt must be in excess of £5,000, it must be unsecured and the receivable must be domiciled in the UK.

 Test your understanding 7

If payment of a debt is not forthcoming what action 'allows the payable to be paid directly by a receivable of the offending company'.

A   Attachment of earning order

B   Garnishee order

C   Administrative order

D   Charging order

Test your understanding 8

If payment of a debt is not forthcoming what action allows the business to be paid directly by the receivable's employer out of his/her/their pay packet:

A   Attachment of earning order

B   Garnishee order

C   Administrative order

D   Charging order

5   Bankruptcy and liquidation

5.1   Introduction

Supplying goods or services to a customer is an **unsecured debt** and if the customer becomes insolvent then often little or no money will be received. There are different types of insolvency:

- **Bankruptcy** – applies to an **individual** or sole trader who cannot pay their debts (personal insolvency).

- **Liquidation** – applies to a **company** that cannot pay its debts (company insolvency). This could be either a voluntary liquidation or a compulsory liquidation:

    - **Creditors' voluntary liquidation (CVL)** – This is where directors, with involvement from creditors, accept the company is **insolvent** and agree to liquidate the company. This is often the result of financial pressure from creditors and discussions with them. Once the directors accept the company is insolvent, a CVL is often the best option.

    - **Members' voluntary liquidation (MVL)** – This is where the members (shareholders) of a company voluntarily decide to wind down a **solvent** company and extract the profits. This is usually when the shareholders no longer wish for the company to exist (for example if the owner-managers want to retire).

- **Compulsory liquidation** – This is where a company is forced into liquidation by a creditor. Any creditor who is owed at least £750 that is at least 21 days overdue can apply to the courts for a winding up petition (WUP). A company then has 14 days to settle the debt in full or agree a payment plan. If this is not done then the petition will be heard in court, who may then serve a **winding up order**. The company is then closed and an **official receiver** will be appointed.

5.2 Terminology

- The **Official Receiver** is an officer of the Court, a civil servant, who is appointed by the court once a bankruptcy order or winding up order has been issued by the Court.

- An **Insolvency Practitioner** is usually an accountant or solicitor who is in private practice. An Insolvency Practitioner is often appointed by the Official Receiver when there are significant assets involved in the bankruptcy or liquidation. An Insolvency Practitioner is regulated by the Insolvency Act 1986.

- **Secured creditors** – there are two types of secured creditors. Secured creditors with a **fixed** charge (i.e. a mortgage that refers to a specific asset or property) and secured creditors with a **floating** charge (i.e. a loan that refers to assets in general such as inventories).

- **Preferential creditors** – as defined by the Insolvency Act 1986 i.e. outstanding wages.

- **Unsecured creditors** – normal trade suppliers and the HMRC.

- **Administration** – is another mechanism for insolvent companies to allow them to carry on running their business. The process is an alternative to liquidation.

  Administration can be started by the **company, the directors, or a creditor**. A company in administration is operated by an **Administrator** (a specific type of Insolvency Practitioner). The Administrator takes over the running of the company (the directors lose their power) and tries to run it as a going concern while options to prevent liquidation are sought.

- **Receivership** – a company may be able to **avoid liquidation** by going into receivership. This is where a Receiver is appointed by **fixed charge holders** to manage the affairs of the company to try to regain outstanding monies owed to the business and also to pay off any debts owed.

- **Company Voluntary Arrangement (CVA)** – a company who is believed to be viable going forward, may agree a CVA with its creditors. This is a legally binding agreement to pay back an agreed proportion of its debts over an agreed time period (usually between 2–5 years). The CVA proposal must be **agreed by at least 75% of creditors (by value).** The CVA is arranged and monitored by a licensed insolvency practitioner. If agreed the CVA gives the business time to recover and trade its way out of trouble.

5.3 Procedure for Bankruptcy and Compulsory Liquidation

(a) The debt has to be £750 or more (£5,000 or more for bankruptcy) for the insolvency process to take place.

(b) The customer is sent an official form detailing the amount owing. This is a '**statutory demand**'.

(c) If payment is not received the Court is petitioned by a creditor.

(d) A Bankruptcy Order, or **Winding Up Order** (Liquidation) is issued by the Court. Any other legal proceedings relating to the receivable's property or debts are suspended.

(e) An **Official Receiver** is appointed. The official receiver takes control of the assets of the business and a statement of the assets and liabilities is drawn up – this is known as a statement of affairs.

(f) The Official Receiver summons a creditors meeting within 12 weeks of the bankruptcy order and may hand over to an Insolvency Practitioner.

(g) Assets are sold.

(h) Distributions are made according to a strict priority:

- Fixed charge holders are paid first.
- Fees and charges of the bankruptcy or liquidation process.
- Preferential creditors.
- Floating charge holders (companies only).
- Unsecured creditors.
- The bankrupt, or company shareholders (if there is any surplus remaining).

5.4 Consequences of a bankruptcy or liquidation

As an unsecured creditor, the supplier is a long way down the list of payments and in a bankruptcy may not receive the money owed.

If a business does encounter one of its customers going bankrupt there are a couple of things that can be done:

- Invoke a **Retention of Title** clause, if present in the contract. This means the business maintains priority over any goods it has sold to the customer when the monies are distributed (see Chapter 1 for more details). The main problem with a Retention of Title clause is identification of the goods that have been sold. This will not work as well for a service provider or a seller of perishable goods.

- The business can claim **irrecoverable debt relief** (see Chapter 1 for more details). The VAT that has been paid by the business to HMRC can be recovered on debts that have gone bad.

 Test your understanding 9

What is the correct order of distribution of assets if a bankruptcy order is issued:

A   Preferential creditors

B   Deferred creditors

C   Secured creditors

D   Unsecured creditors

E   The bankrupt

F   Bankruptcy costs

 Test your understanding 10

Debt collection policy for Green Ltd is as follows:

(i)   Invoices are issued at time of delivery.

(ii)   Statements are sent monthly.

(iii) Terms are payment within 30 days.

(iv)   Aged analysis is produced monthly.

(v)   Reminder letter is sent when debt is 14 days overdue.

(vi)   At 28 days overdue a telephone call is made and account is put on stop.

(vii) At 60 days overdue it is placed in hands of debt collector unless debt is disputed.

(viii) At 90 days overdue legal proceedings are started.

Aged analysis of trade receivables at 31 March 2010

Customer	Balance £	Current £	31 – 60 days £	61 – 90 days £	Over 90 days £
White Ltd	32,000				32,000
Grey Ltd	24,800		24,800		
Brown Ltd	144,000			48,000	96,000

Notes

- White Ltd went into liquidation a little while ago and the statement of affairs shows that there are very few assets.

- Grey Ltd is a regular customer and the latest invoice is dated 28 February 2010.

- Brown Ltd has historically been a good payer, but there are rumours that the business is currently in trouble due to overtrading.

For each of the above, state what action should have been taken to date, and what further action will be taken. State whether any provision should be made in each case.

6 Communication with trade receivables

6.1 Introduction

This section provides examples of letters that could be produced to encourage payment of outstanding debts.

6.2 Collection letters

Collection letters are a quick and relatively easy way of contacting overdue trade receivables.

Each letter must convey the salient points, namely that:

- the trade receivable is late in paying
- the trade receivable is in breach of their credit terms
- payment is therefore due immediately.

A final reminder may be sent out if there is no response to the first. There is often little point in pursuing the trade receivable with many letters and sometimes a threat of legal action will result in prompt payment.

If further action is threatened, then the business must be prepared to carry out the threat whether it is to instruct solicitors, put the account out for collection or stop supplies. There are various letters that a credit controller may need to send out. These are described in the following sections.

6.3 First reminder letter

The first reminder letter is designed to **point out the facts**, the amount outstanding and as a reminder or encouragement to pay the amount due very soon. As with all letters to customers, it must be courteous and succinct as well as firm.

The first reminder letter will be sent out when the debts are a certain amount overdue. The timescale of the reminder letter will depend upon company policy towards debt collection but might be sent out (for example) 7 days after a debt becomes overdue. Therefore, if an invoice is sent to a customer with 30-day credit terms then the first reminder letter will be sent out 37 days after the invoice was sent out.

The first reminder letter will normally be sent to the person with day-to-day responsibility for payment of payables rather than more senior management.

An example of a first reminder letter is given below:

HOWARD LTD
Dene Court
Hereford
HF3 9RT

6 April 20X4
Accounts Payable Manager
Westrope Ltd
Account no: **021547**

Dear Sir / Madam

Further to our invoices detailed below, I do not appear to have received payment. I trust that this is an oversight and that you will arrange for immediate payment to be made. If you are withholding payment for any reason, please contact me urgently and I will be pleased to assist you.

Invoice no	Terms	Due date	Amount
INV12345	30 days	30 March X4	£2,279.50

If you have already made payment please advise me and accept my apology for having troubled you.

Yours faithfully

Sam Yang
Credit Control Manager

6.4 Final reminder letter

If there is no response from the initial reminder letter then there will tend to be little point in sending a second reminder letter. However, in some instances a telephone call at this stage is useful to clear up any misunderstanding and to assess whether further action is required.

The options for a business are to put the debt into the hands of a debt collector, to take the business to court for payment or to suspend any further sales to the business until payment is received. Whatever action the business decides to take, a final reminder letter must be sent to the customer detailing this action if payment is not received.

At this stage, the final reminder letter will normally be sent to a senior member of the management team such as the chief accountant or finance director.

An example of each type of final reminder letter is as follows.

6.5 Debt collectors

HOWARD LTD
Dene Court
Hereford
HF3 9RT

12 April 20X4
Finance Director
Westrope Ltd
Account no: **021547**

Dear Sir / Madam

Further to our invoices detailed below and the reminder letter dated 6 April 20X4, I do not appear to have received payment. If you are withholding payment for any reason, please contact me urgently and I will be pleased to assist you.

Invoice no	Terms	Due date	Amount
INV12345	30 days	30 March X4	£2,279.50

I regret that unless payment is received within the next seven days I will have no alternative but to put the collection of the amounts due into the hands of a third party. If you have already made the payment please advise me and accept my apology for having troubled you.

Yours faithfully

Sam Yang
Credit Control Manager

6.6 Legal action

HOWARD LTD
Dene Court
Hereford
HF3 9RT

20 April 20X4
Finance Director
Westrope Ltd
Account no: **021547**
Total amount outstanding: **£2,279.50**

Dear Sir / Madam

Despite the previous reminders and telephone calls we have still not received your payment in settlement of the above account total. You have promised payment on a number of occasions but no payment has been received to date.

We regret that due to the above we have no alternative but to consider the Small Claims procedure in the County Court in order to recover the sum outstanding. Prior to us taking such action we would however wish to give you one final opportunity to make payment. We will therefore delay submission of the claim to the County Court for a period of seven days from the date of this letter in the hope that the account is settled. We will not enter into further correspondence regarding this matter other than through the County Court.

Please note that if we are forced to take legal action you may become liable for the costs of such action which, if successful, may affect your future credit rating.

Yours faithfully

Sam Yang
Credit Control Manager

6.7 Stopping sales

HOWARD LTD
Dene Court
Hereford
HF3 9RT

Date: 12 April 20X4
Finance Director
Westrope Ltd
Account no: **021547**

Dear Sir / Madam

Further to our invoices detailed below, I do not appear to have received payment. I trust that this is an oversight and that you will arrange for immediate payment to be made. If you are withholding payment for any reason, please contact me urgently and I will be pleased to assist you.

Invoice no	Terms	Due date	Amount
INV12345	30 days	30 March X4	£2,279.50

I regret that unless payment is received within the next seven days I will have no alternative but to stop any further sales on credit to you until the amount owing is cleared in full. If you have made payment please advise me and accept my apology for having troubled you.

Yours faithfully

Sam Yang
Credit Control Manager

7 Summary

If an individual is made bankrupt or a company goes into liquidation, then the unsecured creditors are some of the last to be paid and may well receive only a small amount of that which is owed to them or possibly none at all. Careful monitoring of and regular communication with trade receivables should keep the risk of this occurring to a minimum.

A collection agency can be used for collection of debts but this often has an adverse effect on the goodwill of the business.

As a final resort a business can bring legal action to recover its debts, usually in the County Court or the High Court.

Test your understanding answers

 Test your understanding 1

Answer C

 Test your understanding 2

MEMORANDUM

To: Sales Manager

Date: XX-XX-XX

From: Credit controller

Subject: Credit status of organisations

Megacorp plc

Megacorp enjoys a high credit limit from our company. However the company is a poor payer and abuses the 60 days net terms of sale. Ways in which the account might be managed in the future include:

- The use of discounts for early payment or cash sale.

- Develop a better relationship with the customer to ensure prompt payment.

- Consider ways of providing a better service to Megacorp to facilitate prompt payment.

Goodfellows Cycles

Goodfellows enjoys a relatively high level of credit from our company, of which it does not make excessive use. It is a prompt payer, with the exception of £5,000 which has been outstanding for over 90 days. Ways in which the account might be managed in the future include:

- Settlement of the £5,000 due over 90 days. This possibly relates to a single item, on which there may be a customer query outstanding.

- Find ways of selling more goods to this customer.

- Develop better ways of managing customer queries.

Hooper-bikes

Hooper-bikes enjoys a medium sized credit limit from our company, which it has abused in recent months. Also it has exceeded its credit limit and urgent action needs to be taken to bring this account to order. Future action should include the following:

- Ensuring Hooper-bikes reduces outstanding amounts below the available credit limit.
- Considering reducing the credit limit.
- Considering ways of improving Hooper-bikes' payment record.
- Considering reducing sales to Hooper-bikes.

Dynamo Cycles

Dynamo Cycles enjoys only a modest credit limit from our company and has a good payment record. In the future we could consider the following:

- Increasing sales to Dynamo.
- Increasing Dynamo Cycles' credit limit.

Test your understanding 3

Receivable	Completed action	Further action
Orange	All action should have been taken.	Orange is in breach of contract as they had not contacted Purple within the agreed timescales. Purple can take Orange to court to seek action for damages etc. It is not possible to use the credit insurance as Orange is a new customer. Provision should be made.
Yellow	Invoice should have been sent.	Reminder telephone call may be required depending on the date of the invoice.
Red	All action should have been taken.	Both debts need to be placed in the hands of the debt collector – there is no dispute. Credit insurance may be possible but more detail is required about length of trading. Provision should be made.

Test your understanding 4

Memorandum

To: Henry Tudor

From: AAT Student

Date: 1 October 20Y0

Subject: Monitoring and collection of debts

Francis Ltd – only 14 days overdue as invoice is dated 16 August and each invoice has 30 day credit term. A telephone call is needed to discuss payment of debt. Matters to note:

- Remain polite and courteous.
- Debt of £8,500 is now overdue.
- Is there any query with the invoice?
- If not when will money be received?

Nicholas Evans – county court judgement has been attained. Methods to enforce this judgement include:

- Warrant of execution.
- Warrant of delivery.
- Garnishee order.
- Charging order.

Shields Ltd – debt is 30 days overdue. Account put on stop and a meeting needs to be arranged.

Outdoors Ltd – debt is more than 45 days overdue. Debt needs to be placed in the hands of a debt collector. Make a provision for this debt.

 Test your understanding 5

Answer D

 Test your understanding 6

Answer D

Test your understanding 7

Answer B

 Test your understanding 8

Answer A

 Test your understanding 9

Answer C, F, A, D, B, E

Test your understanding 10

Receivable	Completed action	Further action
White	All action should have been taken.	As unsecured receivables are low down the list when paying in a case of liquidation – write off the debt (irrecoverable debt) and make a claim to HMRC for the VAT (if applicable).
Grey	Should have received invoice and statement.	No further action required at this stage as the debt is not yet 14 days overdue.
Brown	Both amounts should have been placed in the hands of a debt collector. Legal proceeding should have started for the £96,000 debt.	Provision for doubtful debt as there is doubt over whether the company is going to be able to keep trading.

MOCK ASSESSMENT

1 Mock Assessment Questions

Task 1 (15 marks)

(a) A business customer owes £6,000 excluding VAT and the debt is 90 days late. The current Bank of England base rate is 1.5%. Calculate the interest charge under the Late Payment of Commercial Debts (interest) Act to the nearest penny.

The interest charge will be: (1 mark)

£

The fixed sum compensation amount that can be claimed for covering the cost of recovering the debt is: (1 mark)

£

(b) **The Data Protection Act applies to:** (1 mark)

A   Data about individuals only

B   Data about individuals, companies and government departments

C   Data about companies only

D   Data about individuals and companies only

(c) Zanib receives a letter from Mateo containing an order of 50 kg of sugar for £100.

Which of the following statements is correct? (1 mark)

Statement	Tick
Mateo's letter is an invitation to treat and Zanib's response that she can supply the sugar is an offer	
Mateo's letter is an offer and Zanib's response that she can supply the sugar is an acceptance	
Mateo's letter is an acceptance and Zanib's response that she cannot supply the sugar is a breach of contract	
Mateo's letter is an acceptance and Zanib's response that she can supply the sugar is consideration	

(d) **The essential features of a valid simple contract are:**
(tick all that applies): (5 marks)

Statement	Tick
Offer	
Acceptance	
Invitation to treat	
Consideration	
Revocation	
Intention to create legal relations	
Certainty of terms	
Relations	

(e) Ali orders a takeaway by telephone and says he will pay on delivery.

Which of the following would constitute consideration? (1 mark)

A   Calling the restaurant

B   Handing over money to the delivery person

C   Accepting delivery of the takeaway

D   Promising to pay for the takeaway

(f) **Are the following statements true or false?** (2 marks)

Statement	True	False
Under the Consumer Rights Act goods should be of satisfactory quality, fit for purpose and as described.		
If goods are faulty then under the Consumer Rights Act the buyer can return the goods for a full refund within 60 days.		

KAPLAN PUBLISHING

(g) **Match the description to the term** (3 marks)

Term		Description
Void		An unforeseen event either renders contractual obligations impossible
Voidable		Cannot be enforced by law
Frustrated contract		Can be nullified

Task 2 (24 marks)

You work as a credit control manager for Lamb Limited which uses a credit rating system to assess the credit status of new customers.

The credit rating (scoring) system table below is used to assess the risk of default by calculating key indicators (ratios), comparing them to the table and calculating an aggregate score.

Credit rating (scoring) system	Score	Credit rating (scoring) system	Score
Operating profit margin		**Current ratio**	
Losses	−5	Less than 1	−20
Less than 5%	0	Between 1 and 1.25	−10
5% and above but less than 10%	5	Between 1.25 and 1.5	0
10% and above but less than 20%	10	Above 1.5	10
More than 20%	20	**Gearing**	
Interest cover		Less than 25%	20
No cover	−30	25% and above but less than 50%	10
Less than 1	−20	More than 50% less than 65%	0
More than 1 but less than 2	−10	Between 65% and 75%	−20
More than 2 but less than 4	0	Between 75% and 80%	−40
More than 4	10	Above 80%	−100

Risk	Aggregate score
Very low risk	Between 60 and 21
Low risk	Between 20 and 1
Medium risk	Between 0 and –24
High risk	Between –25 and –50
Very high risk	Above –50

The sales department has asked for a credit limit of £50,000 to be given to Cow Limited who is a potential new customer. The financial information below has been supplied by Cow Limited.

Accounts for Cow Limited	20X1	20X2
Statement of profit or loss	£000	£000
Revenue	4,500	5,500
Cost of sales	3,500	3,800
Gross profit	1,000	1,700
Distribution costs	1,050	1,150
Administration costs	1,000	1,000
Operating profit	–1,050	–450
Finance cost	100	50
Profit before taxation	–1,150	–500
Tax	0	0
Profit for the year	–1,150	–500

Statement of financial position	20X1	20X2
	£000	£000
Non-current assets		
Tangible assets	2,200	2,500
Current assets		
Inventory	900	750
Trade receivables	1,000	850
Cash and cash equivalents	50	400
	1,950	2,000
Total assets	**4,150**	**4,500**

Equity		
Share capital	200	1,350
Retained earnings	850	850
	1,050	2,200
Non-current liabilities		
Loan	1,000	500
Current liabilities		
Trade payables	2,100	1,800
Total equity and liabilities	**4,150**	**4,500**

(a)   **Complete the table below by calculating the indicators (to 2 decimal places) and the credit rating for 20X1 and 20X2 for Cow Limited**   (18 marks)

Cow Limited	Indicator	Rating	Indicator	Rating
Year	20X1		20X2	
Operating profit margin %				
Interest cover				
Current ratio				
Gearing %				

Rating	Decision
Very low or low risk current year and very low risk or low risk previous year	Accept
Very low or low risk current year and medium risk previous year	Accept
Very low or low risk current year and high or very high risk previous year	Request latest management accounts and defer decision
Very high risk or high risk current year	Reject
Medium risk current year and medium, low or very low risk previous year	Accept
Medium risk current year and high or very high risk previous year	Request latest management accounts and defer decision

(b) **Based on the results of your credit rating and using the table above the request for credit by Cow Ltd should be**: (1 mark)

A   Accepted

B   Rejected

C   Request latest management accounts and defer decision

(c) **Identify the correct option for each of the following**: (3 marks)

Statement	Option
A rise in gearing could be caused by:	Option 1
A fall in inventory days will:	Option 2
A rise in the gross profit margin could be due to:	Option 3

Option 1	Tick
Raising new finance via a share issue	
Taking out a new loan	
Repaying a loan	

Option 2	Tick
Usually improve liquidity	
Usually worsen liquidity	
Usually have no impact on liquidity	

Option 3	Tick
Making savings on administration costs	
Offering promotional discounts to customers	
Changing to a cheaper supplier for materials	

(d) **Which TWO of the following sources of information would be most appropriate for assessing new credit customers**: (2 marks)

A   Aged receivable listings

B   Trade references

C   Aged payable information

D   Latest financial statements

E   Purchasing manager's knowledge

Task 3 (25 marks)

Chicken Limited has been trading with Lamb Limited for several years and has, until recently, always paid to terms. Following several late payments the directors have now contacted Lamb Limited to request an increase in its credit limit from £50,000 to £100,000. Chicken Limited has supplied the accounts below.

| Chicken Limited | 20X1 | 20X2 | Statement of financial | 20X1 | 20X2 |
Statement of profit or loss	£000	£000	position	£000	£000
Revenue	6,000	6,500	**Non-current assets**		
Cost of sales	3,800	4,600	Property, plant and equipment	4,350	7,050
Gross profit	**2,200**	**1,900**	**Current assets**		
Distribution costs	850	850	Inventory	550	1,200
Administration costs	600	600	Trade receivables	800	1,300
Operating profit	**750**	**450**	Cash	300	100
Finance cost	250	500		1,650	2,600
Profit before taxation	**500**	**−50**	**Total assets**	**6,000**	**9,650**
Tax	150	0	**Equity**		
Profit for the year	**350**	**−50**	Share capital	100	100
			Retained earnings	2,500	2,450
				2,600	2,550
			Non-current liabilities		
			Long term loans	2,000	5,000
			Current liabilities		
			Trade payables	1,400	2,100
			Total equity and liabilities	**6,000**	**9,650**

Additional information supplied by the sales department after a visit to Chicken Limited:

Chicken Limited has recently acquired several new large customers and therefore purchased new assets with long term loans to ensure that forecast sales demands can be met. The contracts with the new customers were only completed in the second half of the year, and it is expected that sales will continue to increase in 20X2 with little increase in costs because the new machines have resulted in a reduction in variable cost per unit.

The directors of Chicken Limited expect a profit after tax in 20X3 of around £500,000. In anticipation of orders for 20X3, Chicken Limited significantly increased its inventory levels at the end of 20X2.

Chicken Limited	Indicator	Indicator
Year	20X1	20X2
Operating profit margin %	12.5	6.92
Interest cover	3.00	0.90
Current ratio	1.18	1.24
Trade payables payment period in days	134.47	166.63
Trade receivables collection period in days	48.67	73.00
Inventory holding period in days	52.83	95.22
Gearing %	43.48	66.23

(a)   **Write a brief note to explain whether Chicken Limited is overtrading by stating the signs of overtrading and considering Chicken Limited's indicators.**   (7 marks)

(b) **Write a report considering all the information and decide whether Chicken Limited should be given extended credit terms.**

(18 marks)

Task 4 (12 marks)

A company's terms of payment are 30 days. It is offering a discount of 1% for payment within 15 days.

(a) **Calculate the following to two decimal places** (3 marks)

The simple annual interest rate of the discount ☐ %

The compound annual cost of the discount ☐ %

(b) Yusif is looking to improve his cash flow and has been considering various financial products. Yusif has forecast sales of £54,000 for the following year.

A finance company has offered to provide a facility where Yusif can be advanced 80% of his invoiced sales. The finance company will not administer the sales ledger.

Yusif can borrow: (1 mark)

£ ☐

This is an example of: (1 mark)

A   Factoring

B   Credit insurance

C   Invoice discounting

D   Settlement discounting

A receivable owes a balance of £36,000 including VAT. The account is on stop. Attempts to contact the customer by telephone and letter have been unsuccessful. The account is credit insured – 75% of the value of the debt is insured.

(c) **Complete the sentence:** (3 marks)

Contact the credit insurer to make a claim for £ ☐

Make a provision for £ ☐

Claim from the HMRC VAT of £ ☐

Hans has received a letter from the liquidator of Leia Ltd. The liquidator has indicated that all unsecured creditors of Leia will receive a payment of 2.8p in the pound (£) later in the year. Hans is owed £4,500 by Leia.

(d) **Calculate the following amounts** (Ignore VAT. Show your answers to the nearest penny)

How much should Hans write off as an irrecoverable debt?

£ _____

(1 mark)

How much will Hans will receive from Leia?

£ _____

(1 mark)

Slide Ltd receives payments from customers 30 days after the month end. A 2% prompt payment discount will be offered from month 7 to customers who pay in the same month. It is expected that 80% of customers will take advantage of the discount.

Expected sales revenue per month is as follows:

Month	Sales revenue
6	£60,000
7	£70,000
8	£80,000

(e) **Expected cash receipts in month 8 will be:** (2 marks)

£ _____

Task 5 (12 marks)

(a) **The normal remedy for breach of contract due to non-payment of the debt is:** (1 mark)

  A   An action for specific performance

  B   An action for price

  C   An action for remedy

  D   An action for the goods

(b) **Complete the following sentences with the phrases below to describe the bankruptcy procedure:** (6 marks)

The debt has to be £ ☐ or more for the insolvency process to take place. The customer is sent a ☐

If payment is not received the Court is petitioned by a creditor.

A ☐ is issued by the Court. Any other legal proceedings relating to the receivable's property or debts are suspended.

An ☐ is appointed and takes control of the assets of the business and a ☐ is drawn up.

The ☐ summons a creditors' meeting within 12 weeks of the ☐ and may hand over to an. ☐

Assets are sold and distributions are made according to a strict priority.

Phrase options (they can be used more than once):

£5,000	Administrator
£500	Winding-up order
Statutory demand	Creditors
Bankruptcy order	Retention of title
Official Receiver	Insolvency Practitioner
Statement of affairs	Receivership

(c) **Retention of title is:** (1 mark)

Statement	Tick
The right of the purchaser to retain ownership of the goods received	
The right of the seller to retain ownership of the goods until a cheque has been posted	
The right of the seller to retain ownership of the goods until payment is made	
The right of the purchaser to expect that title is retained by the seller even when payment has been received	

(d) Ben has a customer, Jerry Limited, who refuses to pay an outstanding amount of £500.

Which of the following will deal with any action taken by Ben to enforce the repayment of the debt? (1 mark)

A   The High Court

B   Multi track

C   Small claims track

D   Fast track

(e) **Legal action can be taken against a customer for non-payment of an invoice when:** (1 mark)

A   There is a contract in existence and the non-payment is a breach of contract

B   There is no contract in existence but the payment is still due

C   There is a contract in existence and the non-payment is a misrepresentation

D   There is a contract in existence and the non-payment is a remedy

(f)   Riko has sold goods on credit to Mia.

Which of the following documents will be needed to aid the collection of the outstanding amounts owed by Mia?

(1 mark)

Document	Tick
Aged trade receivable analysis	
Copies of outstanding invoices	
Copies of contractual documents	
Copies of trade references	
Copies of bank references	

(g)   **Organisations often use debt collection agencies because:**

(1 mark)

Statement	Tick
Debt collection agencies have more powers than ordinary companies	
Debt collection agencies can place customers on stop with all other suppliers in the sector	
Debt collection agencies have a right to seize goods from customer	
Debt collection agencies get results because customers take more notice and are more likely to pay	

Task 6 (12 marks)

Standard Ltd manufactures and supplies wood beams. It also assembles and supplies bespoke beds made to individual customer specifications. VAT is charged at the standard rate on all supplies.

Payment terms are 30 days from the invoice date.

Standard has credit insurance for certain named customer accounts.

You work in the credit control department of Standard. Today's date is 31 July.

(a) **Review the Information provided for each customer below and prepare comments and an action plan for dealing with the outstanding amounts due to Standard.**

Your action plan should include a summary of the options available to Standard to pursue outstanding amounts, along with recommendations for provisions or a write off of irrecoverable debts where appropriate.

(10 marks)

AJP

AJP is a regular customer of Standard and always pays to terms. AJP is responsible for 10% of Standard's annual turnover. AJP had ordered 10 bespoke beds for a hotel it is regenerating. The order had specified that all 10 beds were to be delivered by 10 June in time for the hotel to open. Standard delivered 5 beds on 10 June. However, due to a machine breaking down Standard could only deliver the remaining beds on 30 June.

The total value of the invoice to AJP dated 30 June is £18,000 including VAT. AJP has complained about the late delivery, stating that this has significantly delayed the opening date. AJP is withholding payment and asking for compensation.

CPP

CPP has an outstanding invoice for £13,200, including VAT. The invoice is dated 1 April. CPP has often been slow to pay in the past, and has given several excuses to delay payment, ranging from being unable to trace any of the original documentation to the authorised cheques signatory being away. Standard has supplied CPP with copies of all relevant documentation and, in accordance with the credit control policy, is now about to instruct a debt collection agency or commence legal action.

The HR director has asked you to refrain from sending the debt collectors or instructing solicitors because the Managing Director of CPP is the president of the local chess club. She wishes to join this club, and she is concerned that any unpleasant tension will affect her application.

Standard has had some problems with certain customer accounts following a computer virus. The accounts department has managed to recover the following details relating to the account of the customer RWP:

- Balance at 1 June: £12,000

- Invoices raised: 8 June £8,000 net of VAT, 15 July £11,400 including VAT

- Credit notes issued: 25 June £1,800 including VAT, 23 Jul £900 including VAT

- Late payment charge processed in June relating to an overdue invoice from March £100

- Balance at 30 June: £4,000

(b) **Calculate the monies received from RWP in June.**

(2 marks)

2 Mock Assessment Answers

Task 1

(a) **£168.66**

£6,000 × 1.2 (add VAT) × 9.5% (base rate plus 8%) × 90 ÷ 365

A fixed sum compensation of **£70** can be claimed.

(b) **A** Data about individuals only

(c)

Statement	Tick
Mateo's letter is an invitation to treat and Zanib's response that she can supply the sugar is an offer	
Mateo's letter is an offer and Zanib's response that she can supply the sugar is an acceptance	✓
Mateo's letter is an acceptance and Zanib's response that she cannot supply the sugar is a breach of contract	
Mateo's letter is an acceptance and Zanib's response that she can supply the sugar is consideration	

(d)

Statement	Tick
Offer	✓
Acceptance	✓
Invitation to treat	
Consideration	✓
Revocation	
Intention to create legal relations	✓
Certainty of terms	✓
Relations	

(e) **D** Promising to pay for the takeaway

(f)

Statement	True	False
Under the Consumer Rights Act goods should be of satisfactory quality, fit for purpose and as described.	✓	
If goods are faulty then under the Consumer Rights Act the buyer can return the goods for a full refund within 60 days.		✓

Buyers have 30 days to return the goods for a full refund, not 60 days.

(g)

Term	Description
Void	Cannot be enforced by law
Voidable	Can be nullified
Frustrated contract	An unforeseen event either renders contractual obligations impossible

Task 2

(a)

Cow Limited	Indicator	Rating	Indicator	Rating
Year	20X1		20X2	
Operating profit margin %	–23.33	–5	–8.18	–5
Interest cover	0	–30	0	–30
Current ratio	0.93	–20	1.11	–10
Gearing %	48.78	10	18.52	20
		–45		–25

(b)   Based on the results of your credit rating and using the table above the request for credit by Cow Limited should be:

B   Rejected

(c)   **Identify the correct option for each of the following**:

Statement	Option
A rise in gearing could be caused by:	Option 1
A fall in inventory days will:	Option 2
A rise in the gross profit margin could be due to:	Option 3

Option 1	Tick
Raising new finance via a share issue	
Taking out a new loan	✓
Repaying a loan	

Option 2	Tick
Usually improve liquidity	✓
Usually worsen liquidity	
Usually have no impact on liquidity	

Option 3	Tick
Making savings on administration costs	
Offering promotional discounts to customers	
Changing to a cheaper supplier for materials	✓

(d)   **B** and **D** Trade references and the latest financial statements

Task 3

Chicken Limited

(a)

The signs of overtrading are as follows:

• Rapidly increasing sales revenue normally linked to extended credit terms.

• Reduced gross and operating margins.

• Increased inventory and trade receivables days.

• Reduction in cash or an increase in overdraft.

• Increased trade payable days.

Chicken Limited's performance indicators:

• Revenue has increased by 8%.

• Operating profit margin has declined.

• Gross profit margin has also declined (20X1 = 37% and 20X2 = 29%).

• Inventory levels have more than doubled from X1 to X2 and the holding period has increased by 42 days.

• Trade receivables have increased by 63% from X1 to X2 and the collection period has increased by about 24 days.

• Cash has reduced but is still positive.

• Trade payables have increased by 50% and the payment period has increased by 33 days.

It is possible that Chicken Limited is overtrading.

(b)

Profitability

The revenue has grown but the profitability has declined. Interest cover has fallen significantly.

These are both warning signs but the company has recently purchased new assets using a long term loan. This could be the explanation.

Liquidity

The current ratio has improved but this is explained by the increase in receivables and inventory rather than cash. Receivables and inventory are less liquid than cash.

Trade payables have also increased but this may be distorted by the purchase of inventory to meet increased orders.

Debt (Borrowing)

Gearing has significantly increased but this is due to the loan taken out to purchase the new machinery.

There is no overdraft in use.

The bank has provided this company with a loan which is a good sign. It may be necessary to check how much security the company has offered the bank to secure this loan.

Summary

There are some worrying indicators for Chicken Limited and it would appear that Chicken Limited is now higher risk than it was previously.

A meeting could be set up with the company to discuss the extension of the credit limit to see more up to date accounts.

If the more up to date accounts show that the anticipated orders are coming in then the extension could be considered.

Chicken Limited is still liquid with cash in the bank at the year end.

There are certain factors in its favour. These include:

- A good trading history over several years, although recently it has made some late payments.

- The expansion plan and the fact that the bank has given loans for the purchase of new assets is a good sign.

- New customers have ordered goods and have indicated that they will continue in 20X3.

- The company is still liquid with cash at bank at the year end.

It is worth considering taking some kind of security over the business or personal guarantees from the directors or to consider retention of title clauses.

NOTE: There is no right decision and as long as the student considers all the issues and makes a reasoned decision, credit will be awarded.

Task 4

(a) $[1/(100 - 1)] \times [365/(30 - 15)] \times 100 = \textbf{24.58}\%$

  $[1+1/(100 - 1)]$ ^ $[365/(30 - 15)] -1 \times 100 = \textbf{27.71}\%$

(b) Yusif can borrow **£43,200**. This is an example of **C** – invoice discounting

(c) Contact the credit insurer to make a claim for **£22,500**, make a provision for **£7,500** and claim VAT of **£6,000** from HMRC

(d) Receive 0.028 × £4,500 = **£126.00**

  Write off £4,500 – £126 = **£4,374.00**

(e) **£76,720**

  £80,000 × 80% × 98% = £62,720

  £70,000 × 20% = £14,000

  Total receipts in Month 4 = £62,720 + £14,000 = £76,720

Task 5

(a) **B** An action for price

(b) The debt has to be **£5,000** or more for the insolvency process to take place. The customer is sent a **statutory demand**.

  If payment is not received the Court is petitioned by a creditor.

  A **Bankruptcy Order** is issued by the Court. Any other legal proceedings relating to the receivable's property or debts are suspended.

  An **Official Receiver** is appointed and takes control of the assets of the business and a **statement of affairs** is drawn up.

  The **Official Receiver** summons a creditors' meeting within 12 weeks of the **bankruptcy order** and may hand over to an **Insolvency Practitioner**.

  Assets are sold and distributions are made according to a strict priority.

(c)

Statement	Tick
The right of the purchaser to retain ownership of the goods received	
The right of the seller to retain ownership of the goods until a cheque has been posted	
The right of the seller to retain ownership of the goods until payment is made	✓
The right of the purchaser to expect that title is retained by the seller even when payment has been received	

(d) **C** Small claims track

(e) **A** There is a contract in existence and the non-payment is a breach of contract

(f)

Document	Tick
Aged trade receivable analysis	✓
Copies of outstanding invoices	✓
Copies of contractual documents	✓
Copies of trade references	
Copies of bank references	

(g)

Statement	Tick
Debt collection agencies have more powers than ordinary companies	
Debt collection agencies can place customers on stop with all other suppliers in the sector	
Debt collection agencies have a right to seize goods from customer	
Debt collection agencies get results because customers take more notice and are more likely to pay	✓

Task 6

(a) **AJP**

Care needs to be taken here as AJP seems to be a customer who places regular orders and provides Standard with a substantial part of their sales – a tactful approach is therefore required. The terms of the sale contract need to be reviewed carefully, as well as delivery documentation, as AJP is possibly in breach of contract if the delivery date was not part of the agreed terms.

Even though part of the order was delivered on time, the remainder was 20 days late. If Standard was determined to be in breach of contract, it would be liable for damages. The amount of damages would be determined based on what AJP might have incurred by the way of costs or lost revenue as a result of the delay.

It would therefore be preferable to meet with AJP and negotiate some kind of discount for the problems and inconvenience caused. This would avoid any legal costs, maintain customer goodwill and hopefully bring about payment of the outstanding amount less any discount. As AJP has always otherwise paid to terms, there is no reason to make any provision or take other action to collect the debt at this point.

CPP

CPP seems to have used a variety of excuses and delaying tactics, while Standard has done its best to prove the amount owed. The debt is now substantially overdue (payment was due by 30 April, it is now 31 July, so the debt is 90 days old) with no apparent reason, even though CPP is normally a slow payer.

A credit control policy is in place to ensure that Standard does not suffer any unnecessary liquidity problems or unnecessary irrecoverable debts. As there is no business reason for not pursuing the debt in accordance with the credit control policy, Standard should proceed to instruct a debt collection agency or commence legal action.

Causing 'unpleasantness' is not a sufficient reason for Standard not to protect its business position. The HR director's personal situation should have no bearing on Standard's business decisions and she should not use her position as a director to influence how a policy should be applied for her own personal gain.

It may be prudent to make a provision for this debt and to investigate whether the account is credit insured.

(b) **RWP: June**

	£		£
Opening balance	12,000	Credit note	1,800
Invoice	9,600	**CASH RECEIVED**	**15,900**
Interest charged	100	Closing balance	4,000
	21,700		21,700

INDEX